Where Are All the Prophets?

Jay Reynolds

Copyright © 2025 Jay Reynolds

All rights reserved. No part of this book may be reproduced, stored, or transmitted in any form or by any means without prior written permission from the author, except for brief quotations in reviews.

Unless otherwise stated, Scripture quotations are taken from the New King James Version® (NKJV®).
Copyright © 1982 by Thomas Nelson.
Used by permission. All rights reserved.

Scripture quotations taken from The Holy Bible, New International Version® (NIV®).
Copyright © 1973, 1978, 1984, 2011 by Biblica, Inc.™ Used by permission. All rights reserved worldwide.

Scripture quotations are from the ESV® Bible (The Holy Bible, English Standard Version®).
Copyright © 2001 by Crossway, a publishing ministry of Good News Publishers. Used by permission. All rights reserved.

ISBN: 978-1-7644489-0-1
Cover design by *Matt Brown*
Printed in Australia

This book reflects the author's theological views and experiences and is not intended to replace personal prayer, discernment, or pastoral counsel.

I dedicate this book to all the Prophets out there who long to be free to prophesy.

Contents:

Chapter 1: the Controversy
Chapter 2: the Consecration
Chapter 3: the Call
Chapter 4: the Crucible
Chapter 5: the Change
Chapter 6: the Coaching
Chapter 7: the Covenant
Chapter 8: the Cave
Chapter 9: the Confirmation
Chapter 10: the Completion
Chapter 11: the Challenges
Chapter 12: the Consultation

Preface

This book is written in obedience to the Lord, who told me a few months ago, "This is what the LORD, the God of Israel, says: 'Write in a book all the words I have spoken to you. (Jeremiah 30:2)

It is both a challenge to the Church and an encouragement to her beleaguered Prophets. I have capitalised the names of the five Offices Jesus gave to highlight their significance in equipping and building up the end-time Church and the Bride of Christ.

If we were to ask what the Western Church values most today, we could be forgiven for concluding that it prioritises excellence, order, compliance, and credibility. In its pursuit of respectability, the Church has become highly proficient at dotting the *i*'s and crossing the *t*'s. But this change in priorities is leading many to ask:

Have we become more concerned with pleasing governing authorities than hearing and obeying God? Have we, the Church, become people pleasers?

Where is the spontaneity of the Holy Spirit's gifts and two or three Prophets being subject to one another? Where are the gifts of tongues and the interpretation that bring revelation and power? Where are the signs and wonders? Where are the deliverances? Where is the evidence of the Holy Spirit flowing freely among us?

The early Church valued discernment, but refused to let caution replace obedience. They tested what was spoken, weighed prophetic words, and held themselves accountable—yet they also expected the Holy Spirit to speak often and created space for Him.

Today, as our churches become increasingly sanitised and risk-averse, many have become predictable, dull, and disconnected from the very communities where God has placed them.

When the Spirit is not permitted to interrupt, the Church slowly loses her voice—and with it, her relevance. We no longer have the authority to affect or spiritually govern our nation.

Without the prophetic office operating as Christ intended, the Church risks becoming what Jesus warned against: *blind guides*—sincere, even confident, yet unable to see clearly or lead others with spiritual insight. Teaching without revelation becomes repetition. Leadership without prophetic insight becomes maintenance.

Scripture affirms wisdom, structure, and submission to rightful authority. But it never presents *safety* as the goal of the Church.

Again, and again, God speaks—disruptively, inconveniently, prophetically—and His people are required to respond. The issue is not whether structure matters—it does. The issue is whether our structures still leave room for the Holy Spirit to speak, interrupt, and for *Jesus* to lead our churches!

Where Are All the Prophets? calls on the Church to examine whether compliance has replaced conviction, whether predictability has replaced power, and whether our fear of risk has rendered us spiritually dull.

It asks whether a Church without prophetic insight can truly lead anyone—and whether God ever intended His people to navigate the times we are in, without those appointed to see. The challenge is not whether the Spirit still speaks.

The challenge is whether the Church still dares to listen.

Introduction

If you are a church leader or have ever ministered from the platform, what do you see when you look around at the faithful people in front of you? Are they just sheep who need a shepherd to prod them now and then and help them stay awake during the sermon? Are they the babies Paul mentioned, who need to be fed and kept alive?

Or is this group of people, an *army*, just waiting for a General who will call them into battle? A powerful body with the potential to dominate the area where they meet, once those organs and limbs start functioning and interacting properly?

Sadly, the Western Church no longer fosters active participation. It placates us with good coffee. We stand up, sing, sit down, nod, smile, and then head home. But Jesus' Bride is meant to be so much more.

Prophets are no longer the loudest voices in the room. They are rarely platformed, received or empowered. Over time, they have learned to stay silent.

They have read between the lines and come to realise that *church* is done a certain way now, and unless they are invited to speak, they better keep that mouth shut, or else they might get a reputation or upset the leadership.

Some were once eager to share what they sensed the Spirit was saying, only to be gently corrected, carefully redirected, or quietly ignored.

Others were warned early on to 'be cautious', to stay in their lane, or to leave such things to the leadership. Believers have begun to believe that the Holy Spirit only really speaks through the leaders.

A few Prophets made mistakes and were corrected—but instead of being trained, they were sidelined. Slowly, expectation gave way to restraint, and restraint to resignation.

The result is a growing number of believers who feel muted and without purpose—not because God is no longer speaking, but because the Church no longer knows what to do with those He speaks through.

If you call yourself an Evangelist, you're simply an overly enthusiastic believer who has become proud because you're actively obeying the Lord and using your gift. Still, as yet, no one has *officially* given you the title: 'Evangelist'.

If you call yourself any office in the church without a piece of paper that says you are, you are proud, delusional and attention-seeking.

Many wouldn't even call themselves Prophets—often because no one ever has. If you call yourself a Prophet, you are staking a claim and probably trying to exert control over the leadership. So, Prophets worship, listen, serve, and submit, but never actually get to do the very thing they were born for.

If you are ever trying to find Prophets, look out for those who swim upstream or against the flow. They are the 'voice of one calling in the Wilderness'. They are the ones who can 'understand the times and seasons.' They are those who, like Isaiah, have 'set their faces like flint' despite the rejection, mistreatment and often outright abuse.

We are at a crucial juncture in history. Something needs to change. Our God wants His Prophets back where they belong, and our Church needs them back in position, now, more than ever.

Chapter 1: The Controversy

Few topics create more tension in the modern church than the Office of the *Prophet*. It has always been this way. Prophets confront, correct, and call God's people to alignment — and in a world that prefers comfort over Truth, they are often resisted, misunderstood, or ignored.

Some churches silence all prophetic voices out of fear, while others try to control them. Still others mindlessly follow Prophets, failing to test the fruit of their hearts and the accuracy of their words. The result is a church body that is disjointed, weakened and deceived.

Our own bodies should be a constant reminder of God's will for *His* body. Paul wrote: "We always carry around in our body the death of Jesus, so that the life of Jesus may also be revealed in our body."

And as an ex Judo fighter and rugby player I carry about in my body the consequences of mistreatment and injury which reminds me of the passage in 1 Corinthians 12 that speaks of painful suffering in Jesus' body: "...if one part of the body suffers, all the parts suffer with it; if a part is honoured, all the parts rejoice with it."

While God is certainly emphasising the equality of each gift in terms of its significance in this passage, He is also emphasising that the loss or diminishing of one part affects the whole. He also suggests that if all parts are honoured, the church body rejoices.

It would follow then that if one part of the body is not honoured, then the whole body cannot be truly joyful. The Church cannot truly rejoice, because it is not functioning at its full potential. Part of the body is not functioning well or, indeed, at all.

Having had shoulder surgery and endured 24 hours of not being able to feel my arm at all (which was incredibly disconcerting), I felt something of what I believe Jesus feels when we nullify or remove one part of His body.

As the Word says, "...now indeed there are many members, yet one body. And the eye cannot say to the hand, "I have no need of you"; nor again the head to the feet, "I have no need of you." (1 Corinthians 12) Jesus' body needs all of its parts to be fully functional and working in unison.

Additionally, Paul's teaching clearly shows that church maturity depends on the proper functioning of the fivefold ministries. He states that Christ gave Apostles, Prophets, Evangelists, Pastors, and Teachers:

"...for the equipping of the saints for the work of ministry, for the edifying of the body of Christ, till we all come to the unity of the faith and of the knowledge of the Son of God." (Ephesians 4:11–13 ESV)

Notice the connection: unity in the faith results directly from all offices working together, harmoniously, to equip and build up the church, which is the Body of Christ.

When any office is silenced, neglected, or misunderstood — and all too often it is the office of the Prophet — the church is weakened, losing balance, clarity, and alignment with God's purposes.

The imagery of a hand with all five fingers functioning well lends itself to this idea, enabling us to truly *grasp* the concepts and will of God in each season of the Church era.

In the Old Testament, we read of this strengthening that occurs when leaders cooperate with Prophets and 'build' together: "So the elders of the Jews built, and they prospered through the prophesying of Haggai the prophet and Zechariah the son of Iddo. And they built and finished it, according to the commandment of the God of Israel, and according to the command of Cyrus, Darius, and Artaxerxes, king of Persia." (Ezra 6:14)

Haggai the Prophet urged God's people to resume building God's House rather than remain focused on their own. With this rebuke, correction and exhortation, God's will got done.

True church maturity, then, is not achieved through individual effort, the latest church trends, enthusiasm, or charisma; nor is it by one office of the church compensating for the others, like the Pastor or Apostle who believes he or she can and must do everything.

Instead, maturity in the church setting develops when God's appointed leaders work effectively relationally, complementing each other and collaborating to lead the body toward shared understanding, correction, and obedience. In other words, the unity of the faith comes from the faithful exercise of *all* the God-given offices.

Today, many in the church have lost sight of this truth and have tried to diminish or eliminate the need for Prophets. By misquoting and misapplying Scripture, almost as if it were some sort of cover-up, they claim to love prophecy and say they often prophesy themselves, or at least invite others to do so. They speak as if they are accepting or even appreciating the office of the Prophet.

In reality, however, they are merely describing the activity of the *gift of prophecy*, which is available to all through the spontaneous gifting of the Holy Spirit.

The gift of prophecy is not the same as the calling and office of a Prophet. This gift, which we read of in 1 Corinthians 14:1, that Paul urges us all to pursue, is a temporary gift that any Spirit-filled believer can operate in.

In its context, immediately after 1 Corinthians 13, this verse encourages us to pursue this *gift of prophecy* out of love for others. To prophesy over others is a selfless, loving act. To seek and deliver the Word of God to others is an act of service.

Is it not then, by extension, *loving*, to seek to enable the office of Prophet to function correctly in the church, so that all can benefit?

Other leaders won't openly declare that we no longer need Prophets; instead, they will claim that they can assume the required office of Prophet or Evangelist if the need arises.

In their view, the Church only needs one willing and capable Apostle, Pastor, or Teacher who can assume any of the other offices whenever they choose to function in that role.

This reminds me somewhat of *Modalism*, the notion that God is simply transforming Himself into different modes as the need arises. But this is not our orthodox understanding of the Godhead (three distinct persons, unique in their traits, with individual wills, united as one in love), and this approach implies that Jesus made a mistake when He decided that we need Prophets and Evangelists in the Church.

For those of you who rely on your fallback: 'Well, we just need Prophets and Evangelists in the Church Universal and in that way, we are maintaining those offices', be honest and ask yourself: 'When was the last time I honoured a Prophet and adjusted my life or perspective in response to their proclamations?'

'When was the last time I sought out a Prophet to confirm the will of God for our local arm of the church, which I claim is under this universal covering of Prophets and Evangelists elsewhere in the country or world?' 'When was the last time I invited a Prophet to speak into our decision-making process or allowed an Evangelist to minister freely from our platform?'

Most will have received a prophetic Word from a fellow pastor or teacher who prophesied with the temporary gift of the Holy Spirit, and that is about it. Those words were edifying, encouraging, and strengthening, but were they directive? Did they reveal the future? Did they bring revelation or warning?

We are deceiving ourselves if we do not subject ourselves to and submit to the Word of God delivered through the Prophets.

In the New Testament, we are made aware of Prophets like Agabus (Acts 11 and 21:10), Judas and Silas (Acts 15:32), Phillip the Evangelist's four unmarried daughters (Acts 21:9), and of course, some of Barnabas, Simeon, who was called Niger, Lucius of Cyrene, Manaen, who was brought up with Herod the tetrarch, and Saul (Acts 13:1) – to name a few.

So, we might ask ourselves regarding our own church contexts, as the Lord instructed me to ask back in 2023: **"Where are all the Prophets?"**

If we don't know who the Prophets are in our own churches or movements, then something is very wrong. I brought this prophetic challenge around Easter of 2023 and again in October of 2023. It was confirmed a few days later by an Australian International Prophet, who had a dream and heard the audible voice of God asking, *"Where are the Prophets?"*

This is the question God Himself is asking of all church leaders, and the reason for writing this book. And to be very clear from the outset, Prophets are not missing or non-existent.

They are in every city on Earth, in the midst of most churches worldwide, yet there are tragic and deceptive reasons they are not yet honoured and appreciated as they should be.

Misunderstanding 1:

As with all the callings, the Holy Spirit can gift any of us with a temporary version of that spiritual ability, as He wills.

We might receive the gift of faith, for example, and take steps to pioneer a new venture for God, just as an Apostle would, but once we get started, we quickly realise that we simply want to sustain that venture rather than move on to the next.

We might operate in the gift of prophecy and receive a word of knowledge, and suddenly think, 'Maybe I'm a Prophet' because we accurately shared something that impacted someone.

We could be infused with boldness and share the gospel more than we ever have before, like the disciples in Acts 4, and see the gift of healing and miracles flow through us, as an Evangelist would, and decide, 'This must mean I'm an evangelist!'

We might suddenly have a Word of Wisdom, and on reflection, we reason, 'Well, I seemed to pastor that situation pretty well, maybe I am called to shepherd the flock.'

And of course, with that same gift of Wisdom, we might find ourselves teaching others with much more authority and conviction, expounding a text and gaining revelation we've never had before, and quickly reach the conclusion: 'I must be a Teacher.'

But Paul clarifies that each gift I just mentioned is also manifested as a role or office, and these Gifts and Callings are for keeps, whether we are walking with the Lord and using them for His glory, or if we are out in the world using them to glorify ourselves; "For the gifts and the calling of God are irrevocable." (Rm 11:29)

In the world, Apostles lead successful businesses; Prophets are artists and actors, longing to speak something meaningful with their lives and creativity; Evangelists end up in marketing or sales, finding it easy to convince total strangers to go a certain way or buy a particular product; Pastors take on managerial roles or care work and Teachers... well, they teach.

Before we proceed to misunderstanding 2, it's worth noting that additional gifts can be imparted to us. However, the main point I want to make is that it is God, not us or others, who determines which specific part of the body we will be *before* we are born.

Prophets, being 'Seers' and 'Mouthpieces', serve as the eyes and mouth of the body, and it is God who decides when and 'where' He will place us on planet earth (Acts 17:26) and what specific role we will undertake in His Kingdom. It is also God Himself who insists that Prophets stand alongside Apostles in the church: 'first Apostles then Prophets'.

We need to note that it was Silas, a Prophet and Teacher, and Barnabas, also listed as a Prophet and Teacher, who accompanied Paul as he began to operate in his Apostolic role to the Gentiles.

This model was established in the Old Testament as God sent Prophets to 'kings'.

Misunderstanding 2:

Another phenomenon that pervades the modern church and limits its full expression is the desire to 'maintain control'. This is either rooted in pride or in fear.

Leaders, usually a Pastor or Apostle, insist that Prophets must be appointed by men, and 'recognised' as if divine calling can be conferred through committees or popularity. Yet Prophets are appointed and recognised by God. Apostles likewise are appointed by God, as are Evangelists.

Paul was met on the road to Damascus by Jesus Himself. He duly began ministering as an Apostle without any recognition from the main church, as we read in Galatians 1:

"I did not go up to Jerusalem to see those who were Apostles before I was, but I went into Arabia. Later, I returned to Damascus…" After three years, he went to Jerusalem and, even then, had difficulty convincing the disciples that Jesus had called him to be an Apostle to the Gentiles. He then stated, "I was personally unknown to the churches of Judea that are in Christ."

Paul highlights that his calling was not dependent on man's recognition, and incredibly, he records in Galatians 2:

"Then after fourteen years, I went up again to Jerusalem, this time with Barnabas. I took Titus along also. I went in response to a revelation and, meeting privately with those esteemed as leaders, I presented to them the gospel that I preach among the Gentiles. I wanted to be sure I was not running and had not been running my race in vain!"

It was only then, after *fourteen* years, that the Apostle Paul was finally 'recognised'. He went on to write, 'James, Cephas and John, those esteemed as pillars, gave me and Barnabas the right hand of fellowship when they *recognised* the grace given to me. (Emphasis added).

To provide a more contemporary example, the late, great Evangelist Billy Graham stated that it was God who called him to preach the gospel, a conviction that led him to a lifetime of ministry.

He described feeling a divine call during his late teens, which led him to surrender his life to God's will and begin preaching.

He eventually felt "compelled to preach," stating his sole purpose was to help people find a relationship with God through Jesus Christ. Again, this was God doing the calling and appointing. No one was deciding Billy was an Evangelist, except God.

Billy said, "The only answer I can give is that God called me to be an evangelist, and I could do nothing else but respond to His call." This was just like Paul, who wrote, "...when I preach the gospel, I cannot boast, since I am compelled to preach." (1 Corinthians 9:16 NIV).

This is the case for all of us. Apostles are compelled to start new missions for God, and Prophets are compelled to speak the Word of God in season. Evangelists are compelled to share the Gospel. Pastors are compelled to care for and nurture the flock. Teachers are compelled to delve into the Scriptures and train others.

Even Pastors are called by God - Jesus called Peter to "Shepherd my flock."

Interestingly, the job of appointing Elders, a job given to men such as Paul, Barnabas, and then Timothy, as well as others, was not about recognising gifting, but rather about checking the godlike character of those already called by God. And this is the main problem.

Men, in their wisdom and sometimes a false sense of responsibility to guard the flock, have created their own traditions regarding the trusting and enabling of Prophets and Evangelists to operate in the very same Spirit they themselves operate in.

Rather than invite the Holy Spirit to minister as *He* wills through any of Christ's chosen vessels, they would rather control, restrict or even despise Prophecy and remove the office of Prophet from the church, just in case something goes wrong.

They may even intentionally limit the flow of God's Spirit through the Office of Prophet because they want to remain the sole decision-maker or 'hearer from God' in their church. Even more concerning, they might aim to keep things as they are, 'safe' and unchanged. They do this by claiming that, as an Apostle or Pastor, it is their role to decide who is, or isn't, a Prophet or Evangelist and, in doing so, to 'protect the flock'.

I remember saying to a well-respected Pastor: "Imagine if I just decided right now that you are *not* a Pastor, or that today you can't be a Pastor and that maybe tomorrow we might allow you to be one again?" Would that have changed that person's calling or gifting as a Pastor?

What if we nullified their credential or they moved to a different church movement? Would that Pastor have suddenly lost their gifting? Isn't it more accurate to say they would have merely lost the certificate of *recognition* that *we* bestowed on them?

Jeremiah was appointed a Prophet by God before he was formed in the womb (Jeremiah 1:5). Amos was called into action as a Prophet, while tending sheep and sycamore trees, not after passing through a church hierarchy (Amos 7:14–15).

God set apart John the Baptist for his mission from the womb, and he began functioning as a Prophet without any human leadership or recognition by the institutions of his day (Luke 1:15-17). The list goes on.

The Truth is: prophetic authority is given by God, and it is either *received* or *rejected* by men. As Jesus said: "He who receives a prophet in the name of a prophet shall receive a prophet's reward..." (Matthew 10:41), but perhaps much weightier is the verse that comes before this verse, which sets the context for people *receiving* prophets:

"Anyone who welcomes you welcomes Me, and anyone who welcomes Me welcomes the one who sent Me."

Jesus is saying:

"If they welcome and receive you as a Prophet, they are welcoming Me as I work through *My* Prophets and speak *My* Words to *My* Church." How tragic it is then, when we start telling Jesus how He should lead and speak to His own Church.

Now, as with all callings, the Lord guides us on a journey of growth, but the main point to remember is that we are born with the gift; we don't need to earn it or have someone else give it to us. Men do not determine our purpose on this earth, and we don't require their validation. We only need God's.

Of course, many gifted individuals are unwilling to die to self and pay the price for character development, and so they will never gain the approval of others. However, it is still undeniably true that, in many instances, the issue lies with the character of the leaders who oppose Prophets, rather than the Prophets themselves.

This urge leaders have, to control or have things their own way, must be relinquished. Pride must give way to humility, and any church unwilling to operate as the model churches did in the book of Acts risks functioning like a cult.

We need to remember that the church in Jerusalem sent some of its own Prophets, Judas and Silas, to the church in Antioch, which also had its own Prophets: Barnabas, Simeon called Niger, Lucius of Cyrene, Manaen, and even Saul himself is listed... This was everyday church practice and should be today.

Many churches, particularly in the Western world, prize 'niceness' over authenticity. They focus on performance and presentation over the Power of the Holy Spirit and have moved away from the principles and models of the New Testament church toward something more seeker-friendly, less confrontational, and more relaxed and welcoming.

The Sunday sermon is designed to tickle ears, to keep people coming back, and the church often resembles a nightclub rather than a sanctuary.

So, a Prophet's frustration, boldness, and desire to change things are frequently misread as pride, and their prophetic urgency is mistaken for a desire to be seen or platformed. But it's actually the case that Prophets, just like Jeremiah, feel compelled to speak because the Word of God burns like fire in their bones (Jeremiah 20:9). Their calling is not optional. Their boldness is not a character flaw — it is part of their Spiritual Gift. They *need* to speak, and they need the boldness to overcome the fear of rejection, judgment and discomfort that can come with bringing something contrary to popular opinion.

And God does not require Prophets or anyone else to conform to social norms or to gain popularity. John the Baptist, Elijah and others were not dressed as society demanded. Isaiah, at one point, was not dressed at all! But the average, humble everyday person was keen to listen to John, while the Pharisees, as Jesus pointed out, were not.

And this is an important point when it comes to *receiving* Prophets. On the surface, they may not appear as slick, socially palatable, or laid-back as the average person.

They might be a bit socially awkward or struggle to 'read the signs' to keep everything pleasant and non-threatening.

They could be a bit intense, apparently dissatisfied with the place or circumstances they find themselves in, always looking ahead and concerned about the purpose behind everything. Still, no Prophet in history could just keep their mouth shut!

They say the things no one else is willing or gifted to discern; they voice the heart of God, no matter how challenging that is.

No Prophet in history managed not to offend people, either. Jesus Himself offended folks regularly and was even deserted by everyone.

I really believe that if Jesus turned up at one of our services these days, He would be a genuine problem for many church regulars.

Of course, the Lord calls for Christlike character in all of us, but Christlike character isn't always gentle or agreeable. It is often confrontational, challenging, and unafraid to speak the Truth in love, even when it rocks the boat.

Jesus Himself showed this in His ministry: He healed, forgave, and blessed, yet He confronted hypocrisy, greed, pride, selfishness, and compromise, and He did so with courage, authority, and sometimes a whip!

If you are unsure if Jesus really is all that confronting, go back and read Revelation 2 and 3 and see how He viewed those churches and perhaps even views our own.

Mature Prophets need to reflect the balance exemplified by our beautiful, perfect, confrontational, Lord Jesus — they need to be tender of heart, but unflinching in Truth.

Their distinctiveness can still be unsettling, but this is all part of the divine design to get Truth to where it is needed most, deep in our hearts.

Actually, it is this discomfort and drama around Prophets that can lead to one of two extremes: silencing the office of Prophet entirely, or idolising it above accountability. Neither aligns with God's design.

The prophetic office is not about elevating a person; it is about making space for God's voice to be heard, for Prophets to assist Apostles and Pastors in decision-making. And as we read earlier, to equip and teach others to hear and discern the voice of God.

When the Church rejects or misunderstands the office of Prophet, course correction is delayed, clarity is missed, and maturity is stalled.

This book seeks to restore that balance. To demonstrate how a Prophet journeys with God, learns to hear from Him, and then begins to bring the clarity, confirmation, and demand of God's will to the Church and insight into national and even international matters.

It is an inside story of how Prophets develop — the hidden, behind-the-scenes process that leads to prophetic accuracy, purpose and authority. It is a guide for those who are called, a lens for the Church to look through and gain understanding from, and a challenge to all believers to embrace the fullness of the Body of Christ, as God intended, so that it can function healthily with the office of Prophet fully restored.

Chapter 1 - Reflections:

Point 1: The Church is Jesus' body. He has already decided that He wants Prophets to play a key part in 'seeing' what the Father is doing and 'speaking' His Words to the Body and the world around us.

Point 2: There are lifelong gifts and callings, given by Jesus, and there are temporary gifts and callings, inspired by the Holy Spirit. We are born with the gifts God wills to have on the planet during our lifetime, and those gifts and callings are irrevocable.

Point 3: Prophets are not meant to be '*recognised*' by men; they are to be 'received'. This puts the onus on each of us to resist the urge to control Prophets or to demand that they conform to our own image, before we will listen to them.

We are to 'receive' their gift in whatever packaging it is wrapped in, and when we do, we will receive the reward it brings. Also, when we receive genuine Prophets, we are actually receiving Jesus.

Chapter 2: The Consecration

Prophets undergo intense *consecration*: a setting apart from all else and a setting toward God. Moses lived through 40 years of consecration in the Midian desert after killing a man.

Joseph endured 13 years of torment, being mistreated, falsely accused and imprisoned in Egypt, before starting his 'ministry' at the age of 30.

Ezekiel's first open heaven experience also came at the age of 30 (Ezekiel 1:1).

John the Baptist would have been just 6 months older than Jesus, meaning potentially, both started their ministry aged 30, showing that even Jesus had to 'learn obedience' for a sustained period, so that we would also see the need for consecration and maturity.

In fact, the Lord used the number '30' significantly for me, too. I moved into number 30A on my street when the Lord first began developing my gifting, and at age 30, I committed myself to pursuing God's call on my life into ministry.

Unfortunately, I took a brief detour for a year, as I'll explain later, in chapter 6, but it was by this age that my priorities had entirely shifted.

Maturity is ideally meant to precede public ministry, but all Apostles start churches or ventures that fail, and they learn from them.

All Prophets misinterpret what they are seeing or hearing, and learn from their errors. They may prophesy something publicly when in fact God intended them to spend time in intercession, or they may allow their flesh to sway a Word from God in an attempt to manipulate the receiver(s) or to sound more impressive.

Evangelists may start out as 'Bible bashers', not bothering to find common ground or to ingratiate themselves with anyone, even picking fights or drifting into personal insults as they boldly claim the Truth of God's Word.

Pastors will give bad advice, fail to foresee problems, empower people with hidden, impure motives, and later regret trusting them. They may fail to confront false prophets or those in sin, or to debar divisive people and then feel helpless as the church falls apart or starts to dishonour their leadership.

Teachers will often misapply biblical truths, take them out of context, or not actually teach anything substantive in an effort not to offend anyone.

All of these offices are functioning; God is still willingly using them to some extent, but they are still very much *developing*.

This is certainly true of Prophets. God will give incredibly accurate revelation to Prophets who are far from the finished article. The Prophet Jonah was a racist, and he was full of judgment. He ended up hating his own existence, became depressed and wanted to die, but God let him know His plans for Nineveh and asked him to warn them, so that He could relent from destroying them at that point.

God chose to use Moses despite his insecurity and anger issues, but those old weaknesses cost him a trip into the Promised Land.

David, 'being a prophet' (Acts 2:29) as well as king, was an adulterer and murderer, yet God continued to use him even after his tragic failure and continued to refer positively to His servant; "...David did what was right in the eyes of the LORD, and had not turned aside from anything that He commanded him all the days of his life, except in the matter of Uriah the Hittite." (1 Kings 15:5)

It seems God is infinitely more gracious than we are and doesn't tend to hold things over people the way we do. In the case of David, it's clear the Lord didn't excuse any of his failings, but was far more concerned about David's inner convictions - his core values – rather than his intermittent failings.

The main thing our Lord seems to look for in the case of Prophets is their willingness to do what is right and to obey Him, no matter what reception they might get.

God constantly asks Prophets to do things that might seem unwise, dangerous or just downright embarrassing. To give one humiliating example, Ezekiel was commanded to cook his food over human excrement and lie on his side for 390 then 40 days, to illustrate with his own body and actions what judgment was to come. (His reprieve was that he was allowed to use cow dung – Ezekiel 4)

In my own life, the sting of regret from failing miserably in so many ways certainly motivated me to 'do better.' However, I have also carried a desperate urgency to 'get it right,' to make up for lost time, to make the absolute most of my earthly existence and to obey when God speaks, rather than ignore His voice only to have to revisit that mountain later on in my walk. I believe this is the crux of what God looks for in His Prophets: *righteousness*.

Elijah was referred to as a 'righteous' man (James 5), even though his style was pretty offensive; he became filled with fear and depression, and he didn't seem to show much compassion toward his protégé, Elisha.

It was neither his failings nor his level of holiness that determined God's response to His prayers, but rather Elijah's desire to do what was *right* by the Lord.

This urgency to do what is right (righteousness) is what causes us to pray prayers that align with God's will, which by default will then be answered.

The Prophet is not called because they are special or superior, but rather because they have been placed on this planet with core values that make them desperate to please God and to 'get it right'. This makes them very 'black and white,' often confusing Pastors with their need for clarity on *EXACTLY* what God wants. While they accept that God can guide them back on track, the mature Prophet is not satisfied with detours; they want to get it right the first time and not disobey God in *any* way.

While Prophets can be a bit too serious and often intense about 'getting it right,' there are some positives for them to enjoy too.

It is very clear from Scripture that God entrusts His secrets to His friends—those who earnestly desire to do His will and submit to doing things His way, even if they have significant imperfections.

Abraham was a Prophet (Genesis 20:7), and the Lord expressed His desire to share His heart with Abraham rather than hide it: "Then the LORD said, "Shall I hide from Abraham what I am about to do?" (Genesis 18:17 NIV)

Imagine being considered by God in this way. Imagine God's own train of thought including your name, *"Should I hide from _____ what I am about to do?"* And Prophets enjoy this privilege.

It's not that others won't, or can't hear God at all, as every believer can hear God's voice regarding their own life, but Prophets have the privilege of hearing what God intends to do for others; in corporate scenarios; in the church, in the local area, across the state, the nation or even internationally... *before* it happens.

"Surely the Sovereign LORD does nothing without revealing his plan to his servants the prophets." (Amos 3:7)

Oftentimes, though, we are not being called to announce God's will publicly, but rather God is inviting us to intercede on behalf of other people, just like Abraham, Moses or Amos did: "This is what the Sovereign Lord showed me: The Sovereign Lord was calling for judgment by fire; it dried up the great deep and devoured the land. Then I cried out, "Sovereign Lord, I beg you, stop! How can Jacob survive? He is so small!" So, the Lord relented." (Amos 7:4-6)

Agabus, a Prophet in the New Testament, exemplified an occasion when God *wanted* His will to be shared publicly: "Then one of them, named Agabus, stood up and showed by the Spirit that there was going to be a great famine throughout all the world, which also happened in the days of Claudius Caesar. (Acts 11:28).

He got the download from God, before it happened, and his revelation gave the New Testament church a chance to respond and prepare. I have actually prophesied something similar about the year 2030, and we are personally taking steps to prepare for what we believe are perilous times ahead.

So, the consecration 'stage' is not really a stage at all; in fact, it's a never-ending cycle of refining what God has placed on the inside of us and the formation of genuine Christlike character.

Unfortunately, the desire to get things right can be twisted into pride, and every facet of that deadly sin needs to be addressed.

The urgency to be productive can make us impatient, even suspicious of the leadership of others. This also needs to be balanced. The commitment to Truth at all costs can often leave us saddened by the compromises of others who are supposed servants of God, and we can become judgmental.

So even though God will use unsanctified Prophets to share things on His behalf, He certainly does require of anyone who would truly be His vessel and especially His mouthpiece, a clear transition from glory to glory and a genuine purging of sin. When the Prophet Isaiah heard the call, he humbly exclaimed, "Woe to me!... I am ruined! For I am a man of unclean lips...' (Isaiah 6:5).

I have had this same challenge levelled at me by the Lord on several occasions. And humility is where we start, continue and finish, if we want to serve as an accurate Prophet of God.

One of the upsides of being rejected, going through desert seasons and being falsely accused of motives we don't have is that these hardships train us in humility.

Jesus exemplified this for us on His way to the cross. While the religious elite judged His every Word and scrutinised His actions, desperately trying to trap Him, Jesus remained at peace, continuing His own journey with total obedience to the Father, while modelling humility for us all, leaving it to the Father to avenge Him, exactly as we should.

When John the Baptist was asked about being the Messiah, he told the Priests and Levites he was unworthy even to tie Christ's sandals. Moses, the 'most humble man on the earth', wanted his brother Aaron to speak on his behalf, perhaps because he was unwilling to carry the weight of speaking for God, which incidentally angered God. These Prophets, although bold, were deeply humble.

In fact, all biblical Prophets exhibited an ongoing, total dependence on the Lord for the strength to obey and to honour Him despite fierce, often unwarranted opposition... and so must we.

From the outset, as a Christian, I began reading and studying the Bible every day; listening to sermons and worship music whenever I could, and, most importantly, fasting regularly. In those early months of being born again, I also started reading one of the best books I've ever read on hearing from the Lord, 'Surprised by the Voice of God' by Jack Deere.

I was deeply inspired, but, in keeping with the book's content, I was also beginning to learn how God could speak to me and through me. I'll come back to why this book was so significant shortly.

As someone with a very chequered past, I was keenly aware of how much I had sinned and continued to sin, and early on, I realised that the Lord wanted me to fast extensively to regain authority over my own mind, soul, and body – which we call the 'flesh'.

In fact, as a prolific swearer before being saved, this was the very first area the Lord began to highlight for me as I prayed and fasted. I quickly found that I no longer even liked the sound of those profane words, so I started using substitute words instead until the point where Jesus wanted to heal the cause behind that language.

It makes me wonder, how many other unsanctified Prophets are the kind who 'have a foul mouth' – when they are in fact called to be one of God's own mouthpieces.

During a 40-day fast, I had been asking the Lord why I couldn't really feel emotions for others. Now I am not wishing to glorify my days away from the Lord, so I will simply say that I had hardened my heart significantly while smoking, drinking, doing drugs and a host of other evil things, which meant that I became a depressed, disillusioned, self-focused and hard-hearted young man. As a result, I was uncaring and detached from the emotions of others.

Around the same time that I had begun praying about my hardheartedness, I was also feeling increasingly uncomfortable with smoking, thinking, 'I'm not sure I can keep on smoking as a Christian; maybe the Lord would want me to give that up.'

I then turned this into a prayer and said, "Lord, if You want me to give up, then You're going to have to help me. Last time I tried, I put on loads of weight instead and then started smoking again anyway."

So, I asked the Lord with faith, expecting Him to show me *exactly* how I should go about giving up this time. I thought to myself, *if God wants me to do something, then He's going to have to show me how to do it.*

Although it didn't come immediately, only a day or two later, the Lord spoke to me very clearly about my hardened heart and His desire for me to give up smoking and 'not let any unclean thing enter my body'.

At this stage of my life, having returned from university to live in South East London, I had started spending a fair bit of time with an old friend who had also recently given his life back to the Lord, and we had both been invited to a birthday gathering in North London.

So, just a day or two after I had asked the question about feeling feelings again and with the urge to give up smoking getting stronger, I picked up my friend and announced, "I think God is telling me to give up smoking."

His response was wild. 'Man, I literally wrote that in my diary today, that God wants *ME* to give up smoking!"

We laughed in amazement that the Lord would be so thoughtful as to have us both give up at the same time.

Arriving at our friend's gathering, I found myself sitting across the table from a university student I had never met.

She was talking about her life and all of a sudden started explaining how she had been to counselling many times, but just couldn't let her emotions out... I felt nervous and thought, *Hang on, this sounds familiar.*

She went on to explain that someone had advised her to give up smoking... Again, I thought to myself, *Hold on, what's going on...?*

Then she said it. And it was as if someone had secretly crawled under our table and set up a PA system.

The words came out like they were amplified a hundred times: She said, "because... SMOKING.... REPRESSES...... OUR EMOTIONS".

I was in shock. It was as if 'someone else' was speaking to me. I hadn't told anyone else about giving up smoking or the fact that I wanted to feel real emotions again, yet here she was explaining why I needed to give up smoking.

The reason the Lord was asking me to give up smoking was so that He could answer my own prayer. I needed to remove my drug dependency because it was preventing me from processing my emotions.

A few days later, God spoke in another profound way as He began to teach me one of His regular means of communication: to *say* something multiple times, or, if you like, to repeat Himself through two or three witnesses.

In 2000, in my first job after university, I worked as a Product Designer and began playing soccer locally with childhood friends in the evenings.

The week after that birthday gathering, where I first heard God speak, I had been playing soccer at the local recreation reserve and had just left to start walking home.

As I crossed the road, I realised a guy in a white shell suit tracksuit with a cap, sunglasses and a can of Super Tennent's lager in his hand, was walking just ahead of me.

Unfortunately, he was walking too slowly, and I calculated that I would catch up with him just before turning onto my street. Just then, he yelled something at a young lady who was waiting at the bus stop across the road, so I began to consider what might happen as I walked past him.

With my unrenewed mind, I began to imagine throwing him to the ground and physically assaulting him, but out of nowhere, I had another quite different thought. *"This is not who you are any more, Jay."* And I was convicted. I began praying inwardly for the man instead and slowed my pace to avoid an altercation. *Lord, I pray that you would help him.*

Another thought came: *"You used to be like that."* Again, I was even more convicted, *I'm sorry Lord, please heal his heart, Lord, please save him and his family"*.

At this, the man began to cross my road while I turned right, and as I continued to pray for him, I looked back briefly just in time to watch him casually throw his empty can over the back-yard fence of some unsuspecting neighbour.

But I thought to myself, *Man, that was good. I actually managed to stop myself from being violent and even blessed him instead. Thanks, Lord, for helping me.* It wouldn't be until the next day that I would realise the significance of this encounter.

Early that next morning, I had dropped my son off at nursery and was driving back towards my workplace, praying out loud in the car and asking God to help me figure out how to give up my 20-a-day smoking habit.

Not far from my work, I stopped at a set of traffic lights, and to my astonishment, I realised the man about to cross the road in front of me was the very same guy from the night before, wearing the exact same outfit!

I began praying: "Oh Lord, what do you want me to do? Pray for him some more? Get out? I can't do that here, and I need to get to work…" The lights changed. *Wow, that was weird, seeing him again*, I thought, as I drove on.

During lunch break, I had planned to drive the five minutes home this particular day, so I set off and headed back to work about an hour later. While at home, I had a great answer to prayer regarding finances, and I drove back to work feeling content that the Lord now seemed to be helping me in all sorts of different ways. As it happened, I stopped at the same set of lights I had stopped at first thing in the morning, and the most unbelievable thing happened...

There he was again! The same guy, in the same outfit, just standing there waiting to cross at the lights. By this point, I was getting excited, "Ok Lord, I know it's illegal, but I could just jump out now and speak to him and let the other drivers wait for the lights to cycle through again, but they might start abusing me or something if I do that."

As the man in his white tracksuit, cap, and sunglasses walked across in front of me again, I literally exclaimed, out loud but in a hushed tone: "What do you want me to do, Lord?!" And then the lights changed, so I had to move on, and I continued to pray out loud to the Lord as I headed back to work, "Why did you show me that guy again, Lord? What are you *saying* to me?"

As I was a bit late, I quickly ran into work and upstairs to the design office..., where God answered me.

His word came through a work colleague we all knew to be a chain smoker, so much so that we often ribbed him about taking yet another 'fag break' (cigarette break).

He stood there in the middle of the office, holding a packet of Extra Strong Mints— the ones I used to use at school in a vain attempt to hide my own smoky breath. Suddenly, he announced, "Guess what, lads? I'm giving up smoking!"

My boss and I could have fallen off our chairs, but I was transfixed. I just knew God was about to give me His plan for how I should give up smoking. "Yeah, I'm going to use these mints," he explained. "I'll gradually cut down to 20, then 15, then 10, etc., and when I feel the urge for a fag in between, I'll have a mint instead, it will take the edge off it."

I managed to respond: "When did you decide to do this?"

"Oh, just this lunch time," he replied. "I was in the shop and saw the mints and thought I should give it a go!"

I couldn't believe what the Lord had done. He had confirmed He was speaking, or about to speak, by having that guy at the lights get my attention, and then He had given me the specific answer to my prayer about what method I should use to give up smoking.

My boss suddenly interjected: "Jay, weren't you going to go straight from your home to Beckenham, to pick up that piece of glass?" Although my head was spinning and my heart pumping at the possibility that God had set this up just for me, I managed to regain my composure and said, "Oh, sorry, yeah, I'll go straight away." I also realised that if I hadn't 'forgotten', I wouldn't have seen that guy for the second time.

I got in the car and prayed out loud excitedly, "Lord, I think you've just told me what method to try!"

I then drove down the road to a different set of traffic lights and stopped, waiting for the green light. Looking to my right, I suddenly exclaimed: "Oh....my word, I can't believe this!"

There he was again. Standing there for the third time in a day. Then, as the pedestrian light lit up so he could cross, that same bloke from the night before just sauntered across in front of me.

At this point, I felt a strange sensation, a kind of light-headedness, as I tried to reason how this could happen three times in a row. I was even beginning to suspect he was an angel. I looked to my right, thinking, *But there are no shops that way, why would he just be walking* around, and how did he time it to end up crossing in front of my car again?

I asked, "Lord, do you want me to speak to him? Maybe tell him my own testimony?" But the lights changed, and cars were behind me, so I drove on, shaking my head in disbelief.

That night, I talked with my mother on the phone, telling her how God had spoken, and she agreed that God captures our attention, then confirms His will with two or three more 'witnesses'.

A short while later, I picked up the book I mentioned earlier and began reading the next section, which 'just happened' to be about Peter falling into a trance in Acts 10 and seeing a vision three times.

The author emphasised that God had to speak three times to help him understand what was happening and that it was His will.

Thank the Lord, I successfully gave up smoking back then, using the exact method God revealed to me, and I have never smoked again in twenty-five years. But the lesson I learned was even more valuable, and I have had innumerable similar experiences since, when the Lord has 'spoken' through repeated 'coincidences'. Or as we like to call them, 'God-incidences'.

So, swearing, smoking, drugs, and then drinking became the first strongholds on God's hit list to go, before a host of others that were brought down during those years of fasting and praying.

I would, at this point, encourage those eager to get back on track with the Lord to be willing to fast earnestly to seek a breakthrough, as the Lord directs.

I fasted for 40 days multiple times. I have completed and continue to do various 21-day water-only or liquid-only fasts, 10-day water-only fasts, 3-day fasts, and regular 24-hour fasts.

I genuinely believe that if, like David, our prayer is: "Create in me a pure heart, O God, and renew a steadfast spirit within me." Then we must accept that some sacrifices will be necessary.

If, like me, you have an urge to make up for lost time and want to decide to go 'all in' with God, then 'crucifying the flesh' and starving our appetites is something we all need to do as God sanctifies us, body, soul and spirit.

As Paul wrote: "May God himself, the God of peace, sanctify you through and through. May your whole spirit, soul and body be kept blameless at the coming of our Lord Jesus Christ." (1 Thess 5:23)

So, the 'Consecration stage' began in the year 2000, as soon as I was born again, and it would never be over, but the Call was just around the corner...

Chapter 2 - Reflections:

Point 1: The character of Prophets, just like all other ministries, will develop over time, as the Holy Spirit sanctifies us, leading to increased usefulness. As Prophets submit to Christlike formation, God will widen their sphere of influence and revelation.

Point 2: Prayer and fasting will fast-track your progress as you submit to the Lord and gain authority over your flesh.

Point 3: The actual chance of a coincidence occurring is very low, so it is always worth asking the Lord: *"Is this You, Lord?* What do you want me to see or hear?

As the former Archbishop of Canterbury, William Temple, said: "When I pray, coincidences happen, and when I don't, they don't."

Chapter 3: The Call

The story of every Prophet includes a divine call — an appointment that precedes human recognition or understanding. It comes before or after a season of consecration, or sometimes slap bang in the middle of it.

Few examples illustrate this stage more clearly than that of the Prophet Samuel. God called Samuel as a child, long before he could assert his own agency or gain human approval. He was just a child when God called him to his first prophetic assignment, and all he had done before this was to sleep in the temple and to be dedicated to God's service by his parents.

Jeremiah was just a young lad when he was called and appointed to prophesy, and this is a point I want to raise early on as we consider the journey of any Prophet. God calls, and God equips, but the reason He does so the way He does is that He is primarily seeking obedient sons and daughters who will represent him with integrity.

He will begin to speak through and minister through any Prophet who is ready to obey, whatever their physical or spiritual age.

1 Samuel 2:18-21 reads: "But Samuel ministered before the Lord, even as a child, wearing a linen ephod. Moreover, his mother used to make him a little robe, and bring it to him year by year when she came up with her husband to offer the yearly sacrifice. And Eli would bless Elkanah and his wife, and say, "The Lord give you descendants from this woman for the loan that was given to the Lord." Then they would

go to their own home. And the Lord visited Hannah, so that she conceived and bore three sons and two daughters. Meanwhile, the child Samuel grew before the Lord."

It goes on to say: "And the child Samuel grew in stature, and in favor both with the Lord and men." (Vs 26)

So, Samuel was just a boy when he began ministering, and he was still a boy when the Lord called him as a Prophet: "Now the boy Samuel ministered to the Lord before Eli. And the word of the Lord was rare in those days; there was no widespread revelation. And it came to pass at that time, …while Samuel was lying down, that the Lord called Samuel. And he answered, "Here I am!" (1 Samuel 3:1-4)

Samuel heard the voice of God calling him that night three times, before Eli helped Him understand this was God speaking: "Samuel! Samuel!" The Lord called again. (1 Samuel 3:10). And this time, after his mentor told him how to reply, Samuel responded: "Speak, Lord, for your servant is listening" (1 Samuel 3:10 NIV).

Now the Lord had already sent another Prophet to declare His will to Eli beforehand, but we need to take on board the fact that God Almighty saw fit to tell a little boy of the impending judgment He planned to bring on his own mentor. Why would God do this to a child? Here is the passage:

"Then the Lord said to Samuel: 'Behold, I will do something in Israel at which both ears of everyone who hears it will tingle. In that day I will perform against Eli all that I have spoken concerning his house, from beginning to end. For I have told him that I will judge his house forever for the iniquity which he knows, because his sons made themselves vile, and he did not restrain them. And therefore, I have sworn to the house of Eli that the iniquity of Eli's house shall not be atoned for by sacrifice or offering forever. So, Samuel lay down until morning, and opened the doors of the house of the Lord. And Samuel was afraid to tell Eli the vision." (1 Samuel 3:11-15)

He might have laid down, but I doubt he slept much, and in our Western sanitised culture, we would be accusing God of all sorts. How could He put so much pressure and trauma on a young child? Why is He waking him in the middle of the night?

We would ask these kinds of questions because we are so sure our modern ways are 'better'.

But God chose to use Samuel, even when he was immature, undeveloped, and likely to run a mile in tears, and Samuel obeyed. No doubt he was forever imprinted with the fear of the Lord from that moment on.

My own call to deliver a clear prophetic Word from the Lord to an Apostle would come only a couple of years into seeking the Lord and inviting Him to change my heart, so I was, in many respects, just a 'boy' in terms of spiritual maturity. Yet, the Lord saw fit to use me, too. I'll come back to my 'Samuel' moment later in this chapter, but a bit of background first.

I was actually named James 'Samuel' Reynolds as a baby, because my parents felt strongly led to choose those names, and from an early age, I was passionate about the Lord and His Church. I would weep during worship, singing my heart out to the Lord, and I was hungry to learn about Him and His ways.

At secondary school, I stood up for Christian values and always argued the case for God, desperate to follow the Truth rather than accept the latest theory or ideology. I found it hard to believe that others were content to swallow whatever falsehood the education system was feeding them.

I also loved to argue — and in this, I was often misunderstood. What excited me most was not just being right personally (although that definitely was a challenge I would have to work through), but getting to what was *right*. I just wanted to know what was right — by God. It was an early indication that I prized Truth highly and that I would have to learn the Grace component along the way.

In my pre-teen years, I had two personal traumas that impacted me deeply and had a knock-on effect that led to repeated relational failures as a teenager. I was also bullied through most of secondary school, ostracised by most of my year group and looking back now, I can safely say I was often depressed.

Aged 17, my foster sister was brutally murdered, and my best friend died of cancer just a few weeks apart from each other. I was absolutely livid and became an atheist for nearly 6 years as I raged against God and the world.

Depressed and angry, I married at 19 and had my first child at 21. I then insisted that our son be named after my foster sister and friend who had died. Those next few years at university were torrid and incredibly stressful. At one point, my arm was pulled out of the socket when two nightclub bouncers attacked me, and my shoulder was permanently damaged, leading to repeated dislocations.

So, when I re-committed myself to the Lord back in the year 2000, one of my first ever prayers was a brash, but sincere demand of God: "I want *real* experiences with You, Lord. If I'm going to be a Christian, I want the supernatural experiences the disciples had. I don't just want religion." And God has indeed answered that prayer.

From early on, I found it hard to understand why I kept dreaming about events that later came true. I would watch on and feel like a helpless bystander.

It is true that, like all other callings, Prophets are born with the gift of prophecy, but the wisdom and understanding needed for application must be developed over time, and I had a long way to go.

In 2001, I was 'head hunted' - as I liked to think - by a prestigious lighting design company in Battersea, who contacted me regarding a role I had applied for the previous year.

I apparently came second for that job the previous year and was instead offered the position I held at the time.

I left my first job and quickly enjoyed the new, more executive setting, with company cars, slick suits, and much talk about money, winning projects, and meeting for coffee with interior and architectural designers. But the Lord had an altogether different plan for me there, that would really help me on my road towards Godliness and, well, crush my ego - at least somewhat.

There was one occasion when I was invited to accompany one of the more successful project managers and learn from his approach. Honestly, his slicked-back hair, perfect suit, and Alpha Romeo car all screamed at me: this guy was 'full of himself'.

As we drove around together, I took the opportunity to test out where all his 'success' had come from. I asked leading questions, the kind that suggested he had surely inherited all his clients from others, hadn't he? But as the day drew to a close, with my young toddler son at home and with no desire to hang around with this guy much longer, I explained that I needed to get home as soon as possible, and asked him to drop me at a nearby train station so I could journey back into London.

He had expected me to stay with him until he went home, which would be much later, around 8pm and became visibly agitated at my apparently demanding behaviour. When we arrived at the train station, he exploded.

I won't give you the exact details of everything he said, but in short, he exposed my prideful attacks on his work, made me aware of my lack of experience, and called out my complete arrogance for challenging his career-long efforts to build a portfolio.

I just sat there, going red, feeling utterly embarrassed, unable to respond, knowing that whatever I said could cost me my new job.

On the train, I opened my Bible and read the next passage I had reached: "Do everything without grumbling or arguing, so that you may become blameless and pure, "children of God without fault in a warped and crooked generation." Then you will shine among them like stars in the sky as you hold firmly to the word of life." (Philippians 2:14-15) I felt utterly ashamed of myself.

As a Christian, I was meant to 'shine like a star' and not grumble, but I had spent the whole day trying to undermine this guy in a desperate effort to appease my own ego. The next day, I spoke with him, apologised for my ungodly behaviour and thanked him for the rebuke. To this day, I often tell people that sometimes all we need is a good old 'blast' to bring us down a peg or two.

In 2002, after less than a year in that prominent role in Battersea, London, several key project managers suddenly left the company, taking with them their clients and all the income they generated. As a result, six of us, younger designers, were made redundant by the business.

I was stunned and prayed, *Lord, what's going on? I thought you were promoting me. I thought I was going to be a successful designer, so why would you let me get made redundant and feel so humiliated?*

But the Lord knew what He was doing, and my first prophetic act was about to commence.

As I wrestled with the loss of my job, I reflected on how God seemed intent on humbling me. I also wondered if maybe I needed to change my perspective.

And it was then that I had something of an epiphany.... Rather than ask God to give me what *I* wanted to do.... Maybe I should start asking: "Ok Lord, what do *You* want me to do with my life?" And this was what the Lord was after. My submission to His will, no matter the cost.

So, in that month of 'Gardening Leave' (paid leave until you leave), I began to pray, "Ok Lord, what do You want me to do? If my degree in Product Design was a waste of time, so be it. Tell me what *You* want me to do, Lord."

I also began reading a book called *God Chasers* by Tommy Tenney, and everywhere I looked, every sermon I listened to, the subject of food kept coming up. God apparently wanted, 'the Bread back in the House'. He wanted us, the church, to pursue the 'Bread of His Presence' above all else, and, in fact, twenty-three years later, as I write this, we have just felt God saying the very same thing in our own church setting.

During this time of Gardening Leave, each time I attended my church in Deptford, London, which met in an ex-pub, I looked around and wondered if a café could be opened in the front section of the ground floor. The big windows onto the street were perfect. I began to imagine serving coffee and food and had a quick look at the dilapidated, totally unused kitchen out the back when no one was watching. Within me, God was developing His vision for our church, and this was my first experience of God speaking in this way. An excitement and impregnation of an idea, that we then grow and give birth to, metaphorically speaking. And the timing, as with all of God's Words, was critical.

The phone rang as I was round at my parents' house, and someone from their church was on the line asking to speak to my father. I had just been reading a UCB daily devotional about how ants store up food in the summer for the winter, and how God has given us 'the ability to produce wealth'. (Deuteronomy 8:18)

I was already excited about the prospect of establishing a food business that might be profitable, even *generating wealth*!

My father sat down where I had just been sitting and answered the phone, before relaying to me the conversation: "He's asking if you and I could do a catering job for him, seeing as you're not working and he's desperate. Their caterer has pulled out of a large council buffet on Thursday.... Do you want to do it?" I felt a bit pressured, but then I thought reluctantly, *Oh well, if this is God's idea, then I guess I might as well go for it.*

"Sure, we can do that." I replied, thinking, *This is crazy. My father loves cooking, but food is not really my thing at all. Oh well. I'll try and obey you, Lord.*

Two days later, on Sunday at church, I could bear it no longer and asked to speak with our Pastor. I began, "Hey Pastor, I know this is going to sound crazy, but I think God is speaking to me about starting a café and catering business here in the church. What do you think?" I was embarrassed even to ask, but I was part of our 'prayer and prophecy group', and our Pastor had already witnessed me prophesying accurately on several occasions, so I knew he would take me seriously. His response said it all.

In fact, momentarily, the colour drained from his face because he was clearly shocked.

"That's incredible!" He said, "Only 2 weeks ago, (the assistant pastor) and I found the old café drawings that were drawn up 10 years ago. They were in the bottom of the filing cabinet, and they were the professional blueprints for a café to be built here on the ground floor of the church. We committed to pray that if God wanted a café to be set up, that He would put it on someone's heart to do it... and here you are!"

I was stunned. God had been putting *His* desire in me, and now He was affirming His will and opening the door for me to start a business.

To cut a long story short, after multiple amazing stories of God's provision, in March 2002, I literally brought the bread back into the house and opened the doors to my café, *The Bear Necessities*.

I was extremely blessed to be in a church that actively pursued prophecy and to be under a Pastor who was confident enough to invite prophetic input from me and a couple of other aspiring Prophets to support his leadership.

We would pray and prophesy over certain areas during our monthly Prayer and Prophecy meetings, and it became a regular practice for me to bring the Word of the Lord, which others would confirm.

On one occasion, I had a dream about our assistant pastor bringing a challenge to the church regarding giving, so I went to him and told him, "The Lord gave me a dream and showed me you were planning on bringing a word this Sunday, on giving and that it *is* His will, so go for it!" He was visibly relieved and confirmed he had been stressing about doing precisely that, that coming weekend.

A lot of spiritual growth took place over that next season, as I ran the café and loved on my church and community, stepping out in faith to deliver prophetic words.

As a Prophet who was learning to decipher God's Words from my own, God's priorities over my own and to interpret the many dreams I was getting and prophetic visions and signs, I did come to realise later regarding the Word I thought He had given me about a thriving café and catering business, that it was not in fact a calling on me to 'produce wealth', but rather God informing me that it was Him alone who gave me any ability whatsoever to 'produce wealth'!

As such, I spent the next couple of years praying my heart out for catering jobs to come in, for God to help me earn just enough, and for me to be used by Him, as I ministered to customers, seeing frequent answered prayers and people coming to the Lord.

I realised that my pride had to go, and that I needed to seek God's Kingdom above anything else, especially the pursuit of wealth.

Unfortunately, the financial pressure did not help my already fractured marriage, and we continued to argue and disconnect.

While my then wife was pregnant with our second child, I began praying about what to call him and one morning I awoke after having a dream. In the dream, an older man had walked up to me and said, "Pay attention to your wife's dreams."

So, as I awoke, I asked her if she had dreamt about anything. She said she hadn't, so I was confused.

But that night, friends came over, and we watched The Lord of the Rings, and as the credits rolled on and on, we all started talking about possible names. I even said Elijah might be good, as Elijah Wood's name rolled past. Our friends enthusiastically agreed, and we joked about other options before they went home.

The next morning, my then-wife woke up with frantic urgency. "I've just had a dream she said, and I was told, "1 Kings 17:24". If that verse has a boy's name in it, we have to call him that!"

As she ran downstairs to look up the verse, I thought to myself, *I'm pretty sure Elijah is in that part of the Bible,* and followed her downstairs.

"It does!" She said and read out the verse: "Then the woman said to Elijah, "Now I know that you are a man of God and that the word of the Lord from your mouth is the truth." (1 Kings 17:24 NIV)

I actually took this as a Word from the Lord for me. By calling our son 'Elijah', I was not only confirming the prophetic call on his life, but also affirming the season I was personally walking into.

'The Woman' (my then wife) said to me: "Now I know that you are a man of God and that the word of the Lord from your mouth is the truth."

It was exciting to experience this level of interaction with the Lord regarding my son's name.

My oldest had, unfortunately, been burdened with those two names I insisted he should have, as memorials to my foster sister and best friend, but the toss of a coin decided his second middle name. That name, I believe, God chose. It means 'Gift of God'. I will return to why his name was so important later on.

So, I was committed to the Lord, but despite the dream she had had, my wife at the time was not interested in pursuing God or going to church and tragically, despite our second son being born, our marriage collapsed completely.

Meanwhile, the Lord began to conceive in me the first prophetic Word He would have me deliver to an Apostle.

As my wife drifted away and into the arms of others, the story of Hosea just kept coming up for me. I began to weep at the unfaithfulness and grief I was experiencing, asking the Lord, "Are you actually bringing up the story of Hosea because You want me to share something?"

One time, I was crying out to the Lord, "Am I actually like Hosea then? Please confirm this is *You* Lord." And I went straight downstairs to my friend, who was now a lodger in our house, and asked if we could worship together. He was a musician, and he could see I needed some support, so he started playing the guitar, and we worshipped together.

Suddenly, after the first song, he stopped and looked at me, saying, "I'm sorry, Jay, but I think God is saying you need to be like Hosea".

I was already sick to my stomach at the idea, but it was strangely comforting to think that this suffering might have a purpose, or that God could bring something 'good' out of it.

Not long after, I was up at a place called One Tree Hill, not far from where I lived, where I went to pray most days, and I said out loud and passionately, "Lord, this is so hard, how am I supposed to do this? It's like you're asking me to love someone who is spitting in my face!"

That same evening at Connect group, our leader interjected a prophetic word during the worship: "I just feel like God is saying: 'Sometimes He wants us to love people, even if they're spitting in our face'. The Lord again confirmed this was the 'Hosea season' for me and that He was standing there with me when I prayed those words out loud, earlier that morning.

What paralleled this season was a huge church split in the church movement I had been born into, one that my parents and 12 others had started back in the seventies.

The movement had grown to approximately 3000 people, including many congregations and linked churches, and all of a sudden, the leaders were at each other's throats. My father was now a trustee, and I was aware of the intense meetings going on, so while I was experiencing the sickening feelings of betrayal and unfaithfulness personally and dreading the probable divorce, I readied myself for God's Word to come regarding the church situation. *And it did.*

I had noticed the parallel and began praying that the Lord would speak into the church situation and prevent a church split. I prayed this as I prayed for my own situation, that even though I didn't want to be with my then-wife, the Lord would prevent a split for us too, for the sake of our two sons.

One night, as I prayed, I picked up a book I had been reading. In the very next section, I read that the author, too, had almost been involved in a terrible church split, and that he and all the leaders had gone away together to pray and fast, refusing to return until they had found agreement and unity.

I felt God's weight on the words in the book, so I prayed: 'Lord, if you really want me to share this idea with the Apostle of our movement, then send him to my café tomorrow.' I knew he had never been there before and that it was highly unlikely he would suddenly pop in tomorrow, given all the traumatic meetings going on, so I reasoned that this would be confirmation if he did miraculously turn up…

And yes, he turned up the very next day, with a friend he had invited down from Scotland, apparently to help with all the arguments that were going on.

I was genuinely stunned when he walked in. Amazed at how often God proved He was listening to my specific prayers and that He wanted me to be His mouthpiece in this situation, I, like Samuel, felt intimidated, because in faith I was just a child - I had only been back with the Lord for 2 years. Still, here I was, the son of one of the founding couples of our church movement, being tasked with confronting our Apostle with the challenge God wanted to set before all our leaders.

I nervously greeted them both as they came in, and then, after a short while, asked if I could speak privately with our Apostle, who was the overall leader of our church movement.

The two of us stepped out the back for a few minutes while I grabbed the book I had taken with me to work, in faith. "The Lord asked me to share this with you," I began, and then briefly read the story from the book about fasting and praying and finding unity.

He didn't seem too impressed and no doubt thought, *Who is this young upstart correcting me on how we should deal with this conflict?*

So, I added, "I actually asked the Lord to send you here today, if I was meant to share this idea with you on God's behalf.' He seemed slightly more impressed, then apologised for needing to head back to his friend. I could tell he wasn't moved by the Word of God I had delivered, and this would not be the first time I felt the grief of being a Prophet.

In fact, I came to realise that the grief Hosea felt, the grief I felt in my own circumstances, is the same grief the Lord feels when we betray Him and go our own way. So many leaders will find out on Judgement Day that they grieved the Holy Spirit by hardening their hearts and deciding they knew better than the Lord. So many believers will be distraught as they realise just how much we have hurt our perfect Lord Jesus, with rebellion, manipulation and our stubborn insistence on getting our own way.

As Prophets, our job is to live out or receive the Word of God, and then to deliver it in the tone that Jesus would use. Often, as modelled in the Old Testament (the natural blueprint for all things spiritual), He will call us to speak to Apostles and other leaders in all sorts of settings, on His behalf.

But it is not our job to chase people and force them to respond to God's Word, and tragically, very often they won't.

We can only intercede and pray for Godly outcomes, trusting that, in God's economy, His methods of warning us are sufficient and fair, and that the repercussions are left to Him.

And so, our beloved church, which had seen incredible miracles, many deliverances, rich Spirit-filled worship and incredible teaching and growth in every way for some twenty-seven years, split later that year, with many leaving and only a third of the original church remaining with the Apostle. The leaders did not go away together and fast and pray for unity; they did things their own way.

Towards the end of 2002, after all of this, my parents moved out of London to a small village, in which their road happened to lead to the edge of a hamlet called 'Noah's Ark'. The sign 'Noah's Ark' was at the end of their road, and this story of Noah would soon become *VERY* important to me and even the world.

Their moving out there was actually the beginning of an eighteen-year prophecy that I would not formally deliver until 2020 and 2021, but I'll return to that later.

This next season, from 2003 to 2007, has multiple names in the Bible: *the desert season*, *the wilderness*, *the dry season*, but as Job put it, for me it was more like a *crucible* season.

Chapter 3 - Reflections:

Point 1: God will, at some point, 'call' us into action. It will take faith and humility on our part to respond to the call. Remember that we are simply the messengers. Resist the urge to influence or control the outcome. Once we have delivered the Word of the Lord, we can always pray, but it is not our job to force others to submit to it.

Point 2: Our faithfulness will not always be met with gratitude. We must be willing to prophesy without needing the approval of men, but also with the grace and love of a brother or sister in Christ.

Point 3: Pay attention to the God-incidences in your own life. Are you 'walking out' a prophetic Word?

Chapter 4: The Crucible

From 2002 to 2005, I ran the café and eventually handed it over to another young lady in our church, who took it further and grew it. There were many miracles and prophetic Words in those few years as I worked in the café, interacted with my community, and learned to minister to the public and overcome my fears.

The devil, however, sent along plenty of opposition, including a demoniac who would arrive almost every day to try and intimidate me, writing *666* in the Guest book and several expletives which he also verbalised.

This was a season for me, where the Lord was calling on me to have '*No Fear*', and I wore that clothing brand deliberately at that time, to declare that the Spirit I had on the inside of me was *not* one of fear.

Over the next few years, I continued the catering side of things in a nearby industrial unit, still employing several staff, but definitely wondering if this was really God's plan for my life. While things seemed quiet and mediocre on the work front, I was soon going to endure significant emotional pressure in an intense season of breaking. God was going to turn up the heat in order to sanctify me further.

Although we may not read the details of what other Prophets went through in the Bible, we do know about Joseph's testing season.

As we read in Psalm 105:19, God was working on Joseph throughout this season of apparent delay, even when it must have felt as though God had completely abandoned him.

Joseph probably wrestled with pride as the favoured son; we don't know for sure, but he was able to see God's hand in the entire painful sequence of events, later claiming of his brothers' actions: 'But as for you, you meant evil against me; but God meant it for good, to bring it about as it is this day, to save many people alive." (Gen 50:20).

The isolation of John the Baptist before coming to prominence may have been necessary to help develop a humble heart. If we let Him, Jesus will bring the impurities to the surface in this season so He can remove them, and generally that can only happen during intense 'heat' and testing: "The crucible for silver and the furnace for gold, but the Lord tests the heart." (Prov 17:3 NIV)

Peter tells us again that testing and trials are a given, and that we should even celebrate what God is doing as a result of this season: "In all this you greatly rejoice, though now for a little while you may have had to suffer grief in all kinds of trials. These have come so that the proven genuineness of your faith—of greater worth than gold, which perishes even though refined by fire—may result in praise, glory and honour when Jesus Christ is revealed." (1 Peter 1:6-7 NIV)

And all Prophets will need to submit themselves to this season of cleansing if they want to become vessels for special use:

"Therefore, if anyone cleanses himself from the latter, he will be a vessel for honour, sanctified and useful for the Master, prepared for every good work." (2 Tim 2:21)

It was at the end of 2002, going into 2003, that my then-wife separated from me again and began living elsewhere.

Our second son had only been born in August 2002, and I was grieved by both the situation and the trauma our boys were experiencing. We tried marriage counselling and, in the end, I got personal counselling, which was life-changing, and I hung onto the Lord as it became clear she had no intention of coming back.

Loving someone who wants nothing to do with you is incredibly difficult, but as Paul said, and I paraphrase: 'as we share in Christ's sufferings, we get to know Him better.' (Phil 3:10) As we suffer deep grief, we realise what the Lord Himself felt and feels.

During the separation, we shared custody of our boys 50/50, so as a single parent for half the week, each week, I needed to love and protect them as best I could and to process my own grief privately as much as possible.

I visited my parents most weekends and walked to Noah's Ark and the surrounding countryside as I processed this dark season and wondered why the Lord seemed intent on burdening me with such searing pain and loss.

I knew deep down I had to take responsibility for my own actions, but I still felt hurt that the Lord seemed unwilling to help fix the situation.

Unbelievably, my then-wife wanted the family home, which I had prayed for and seen God deliver to us (another crazy miracle).

Although she couldn't afford to borrow enough to pay the legitimate cost of transferring it solely into her name, I felt the Lord ask me to, 'Let it go', rather than go through the court system.

So, I did, losing out on an additional £10000 that I could have demanded.

I was in such a dark place that I said to the Lord angrily: "If you want me to give up the home I prayed for, then you have to provide another home for the boys and me."

"Also, I only want to be paying what I'm paying now on the mortgage, £500 maximum. And I'm not doing anything. You have to make it happen."

At the time, a young man was working for me whose relative owned and rented a house just around the corner from our home. When I mentioned I was looking to move, he urged me to contact the estate agent and ask if it was available. So, despite my reluctance, I did. It happened that the lady overseeing the house attended my church, and yes, it was about to become available.

We met up a couple of days later, and as I viewed the three-storey house, with its two bathrooms, four bedrooms and two reception rooms, I thought to myself, *It's actually pretty decent, but the rental price is too high at £1200.*

So, I asked if they would accept £1100, reasoning that I could rent the other half for £600 and still meet the £500 maximum cost I had demanded from the Lord. And they agreed.

But the fleeting hope I felt dissipated as I spoke to my mother on the phone. I told her I was considering the house, but had nothing in me to try and find any tenants who might share with my boys and me.

My mother tried to encourage me to be willing to do something, and I literally said, "If God wants me to move, He has to do it; I'm not doing anything more."

"At least just do these two things and then leave it up to God," She said. "Put an ad in the church bulletin and call (our missionary friend) – she always seems to know people."

So, I accepted that challenge, emailed the ad to their church and called our missionary friend. "Hi, it's Jay. I'm just letting you know I'm looking for tenants who might want to share a house with me. If you know or hear of anyone, could you let me know?" She said she wasn't aware of anyone at the moment, but would definitely pray.

Three days later, my mobile rang. "Hi Jay!" It was a young lady from my church, "I just spoke to (our missionary friend), and asked if she knew anyone who might be able to rent us a couple of rooms in their house... Apparently, you're looking for someone?"

I was shocked to hear such precise provision coming my way. "Would you be ok with our family taking the rooms?" She finished.

And so, the Lord provided, and shortly after, we moved into our new house along with this lovely young family from church.

In that season, being without a partner, the Lord was purifying my heart and mind. As I continued to fast and pray, the Lord was cleansing me from impure thoughts and motives and at the same time, I was leading men in our church to do likewise.

But after the family who needed a temporary home (while they sought a new home of their own to purchase) left our shared house, I made the 'mistake' of advertising the two rooms to just anyone.

Rather than keep the house pure, I opted to compromise. But as the Lord says in Corinthians: "What fellowship does light have with darkness?" And although those two young ladies who moved in were very friendly, and we all got along fine, God began to speak to me through my dreams, through conviction, and, of course, through circumstances.

Despite months when nothing had happened, and everything seemed fine, the night came when a total stranger arrived at my home. I woke up with my two young sons to find this guy I'd never met walking around my house. At this point, I realised God's Word is *NEVER* wrong.

We can think everything will be fine, a little compromise here or there won't really matter, but we have, in effect (and in my case, quite literally), opened the door to compromise and problems. It wasn't long before I had to ask those young ladies to move out, and this time, I rented the rooms to two lovely young Christian ladies who were wonderful.

This was just one of many stories during those 5 years, in which the Lord used the circumstances I was in to test and purify my heart and mind.

However, one of the biggest tests came one night, when the girls who were living with me asked if they could store some items in our attic. I duly climbed up the ladder into the dark attic of our house, only to find a huge stash of pornographic materials, DVDs, magazines, etc.

Apparently, as we established later, unbeknownst to the owners, one of the previous tenants had been working in that industry. It was unbelievable.

The temptation of that box to take the route of gratifying my flesh was so strong because, as we know, the devil waits for 'an opportune moment'. When we are at our lowest, he comes along, tempting us to dive headlong into sin.

So as soon as I found the box, something in me said, *"Run!"* Just like Joseph with Potiphar's wife. I nearly fell, as I quickly climbed down the ladder in a panic, my heart racing. *I need to ring my Pastor,* I thought. *I need to get this box out of here before I fall into sin.*

At the time, I had begun to lead the Evening Service at our church. Drunks and drug addicts who were living on the local streets would often join us, and as I have a strong sense of smell, I really struggled to deal with the affronting reek of alcohol and body odour.

We had begun feeding them, and over the years, this ministry expanded and still runs to this day, as they just kept coming.

I asked the Lord to give me a heart for these people, even though, in my flesh, the smell repulsed me. So, the Lord did something supernatural in me, enabling me to hug those guys warmly, no longer affected by the smell. This was truly amazing!

As it was Saturday night when I found the box, my Pastor and I decided I should bring it to church for the Evening Service the following day. We used the opportunity to invite other men, including the street guys, to help burn those DVDS and magazines out in the back yard as we all committed ourselves to a life of purity and of breaking the stronghold of lust.

It was an incredible moment, and I felt the Lord's pleasure at our response to the situation. Like I said, though, this testing season was intense. Our bodily urges can be powerful, and the only solution is to '*Flee*' rather than try to hang around and resist temptation.

Our victory comes as we starve the flesh and all its desires - as we 'Buffet our bodies' as Paul said, which is to *beat it unto submission*, not serve it a three-course meal!

The Lord knew that box was up there in the loft. Like Abraham, God wanted to see what I would do when I found it and if the cost seemed too high. Abraham had to decide if he would plunge that knife into his own son and give up his apparent legacy. I had to decide if I would backslide and give up years of progress.

When God tested Joseph, He knew he would be tempted to give in and compromise, but Prophets have to learn to love the Truth, hate falsehood, and never, *ever* compromise.

This is because God will not continue to speak through those who are open to other spirits, to sin and to compromise.

As we read in Acts 8, Simon the sorcerer wanted the power, without being willing to walk the road of submission to the Lord, and Peter rebuked him for it. Balaam, a mercenary Prophet, was warned by a speaking donkey that He was heading into judgment, so instead of cursing Israel, he made the life-saving choice to bless God's people.

The *crucible* is the season Prophets go through to test their motives and remove the mixture of impurities that would otherwise taint the prophetic words they are commissioned to deliver.

We need to operate from a heart-motive of love, rather than a mixture of control, fear, or pride. We can't love and enjoy the power of prophecy without loving and enjoying the Source of that power: *Jesus!*

In November 2006, I had an incredibly clear and accurate dream of Steve Irwin - the Australian national treasure - swimming in the sea over a sting ray and saw him being killed by it, as its barb went into his chest. I awoke in shock and thought, *What was that about?!*

Later that day, I found out that Steve Irwin had indeed died in this very unusual way.

For some reason, the Lord had shown me in a dream a literal event I could not possibly have known about, involving an Australian icon.

What link did I have to Australia? I mused as I found out the dream was 100% accurate.

A few months later, I was prophesied over by a Prophet from the North of England, and he prophesied I would end up with a very strong connection to the other side of the world; he could see a globe and both sides of it. The UK and Australia.

Little did I know I would end up married to an Australian, living here for the last 5 years, and even becoming an Australian citizen. Back then, I had no idea, but God already saw the connection.

In 2006, we, as a church, were made aware that although our previous Apostle and their team had allowed us to continue leasing the church building (even though we had gone 'independent' after the church split), they were planning to sell it. We would have to find another venue soon.

So, the Lord spoke to me in a dream. I dreamt of our Pastor walking towards a red brick church building (which I later found out was one he used to drive past on the way into our church and always dreamed of leading a church in), and I saw another church leadership team inviting him to make a proposal to them, regarding their building. In the dream, I heard them saying they wanted to give us their church building.

By now, I had learned to act on my dreams, so I delivered God's prophetic declaration to our Pastor and shared with him what was going to happen.

A week or so later, a pastor from a small church down the road, which owned the very large Shaftesbury Centre church building, arrived to speak with our Pastor and, after hearing out our Pastor's heart, to offer us their building...!

This was another very specific and timely Word from the Lord. In the dream, God was showing our Pastor that this would be the building he would want to minister in.

It was also evident from my dreams at this time that the Lord was speaking to me specifically about my personal circumstances. On one occasion, I actually met the Lord in a dream, and He helped me let go of the idea that my wife would return. He was showing me that she had made her decision, and even though Hosea received his wife back, that this was not going to be the case for me.

As such, I realised that God often prophesies something that depends on how people respond.

He doesn't change His mind; rather, He predetermines what He will do based on our response. "If they repent, I will relent", as Jonah learned.

The Prophet has to learn to let God be God and to trust Him with the future, even when people don't respond to the Word we bring or to what He is speaking to them.

It was around this time that I started experiencing God-incidences related to name changes. As I was about to get some new business cards for my catering business, I decided to begin going by the nickname I liked.

Although I was officially named 'James', my nickname since early childhood had been 'Jamie', but my father always called me 'Jay', which I personally preferred. I asked everyone I knew to start calling me 'Jay' from then on.

Shortly after, I discovered the boys' mum had found a new partner who went by my previous nickname.

I felt the love of Father God as He eased me into my new season and new identity. I was relieved I would now only hear the affectionate nickname my earthly father used, and it felt as if my Father in Heaven was making sure I would still sense His love for me during this challenging transition.

Sadly, though, accepting that the boys' mum was permanently moving on with another guy meant that the hope I had held onto - that I would get to stay 100% part of my sons' lives - was dashed. On several occasions, I wept on the floor in the foetal position, crying so hard I felt I could die.

The pain was so intense and the sadness so overwhelming. I loved my sons so much, and the thought of another man raising them instead of me, for half their lives, broke my heart.

In this season, I understood what God meant when He spoke of divorce in the Bible, not just between individuals, but between Himself and His beloved people. Our God is deeply emotional.

He is a jealous God, we belong to Him, and when we stray after other lovers, the gods of entertainment, sport, money, sex or anything else that is self-gratifying, He hates it. His heart is genuinely impacted.

When the New Testament says that we grieve the Holy Spirit by despising prophecy, it really means exactly that. He experiences grief because we refuse to submit to His ways and want to control and restrict His activity.

Shortly after all of this, in 2007, my eldest son began refusing food. Initially, I thought this must be a cold; he seemed to have a sore throat, but it didn't take long before I was back at the doctor's, saying something was really wrong.

I railed against the doctor's passivity, who wanted to send us away for a few more weeks, and I insisted that my son be seen immediately by an ENT (Ear, Nose, and Throat specialist), saying forcefully, "Something is badly wrong, it's not a cold!"

Soon after, we sat with the ENT, and as he looked down my son's throat, his face went pale. "We need to take him in today. We need some scans done urgently," he said with a grave look on his face....

It wasn't long before we discovered the unbelievable news that my beautiful son, who had just turned 8, had stage 2 non-Hodgkin's lymphoma in his throat. *CANCER.*

It seemed to me that he had not been able to speak about the situation he was in emotionally, and now his body reflected this reality.

It was like some sort of sick, cosmic joke. I was going through a separation, grieving and weeping regularly at the prospect of losing access to half of my sons' lives and heading for divorce, and now my beloved older son had a lump of cancer the size of an egg, behind his throat, which could kill him. My poor boys, aged 8 and 4, were suddenly enveloped in talk of chemotherapy, awful side effects on the body of my oldest and days apart as their mum and I alternated halves of the week at the Royal Marsden Hospital with our eldest.

At the time, I handed over my business to my full-time staff member but kept my van. I stayed in the hospital with my oldest for the first part of the week, for many weeks, but work as a courier or man-and-van would come in every Thursday, Friday, or Saturday without fail - the days I was back home and able to work.

So, despite the challenging situation, the Lord kept us going, and somehow, I managed to support my two sons.

I wanted to hear from the Lord on what was going on and battled to work out why a good God would really allow such horrendous things to happen to His beloved children. But it was in this season that I learned to war and to refuse to accuse God falsely.

I was reading an incredible book at the time, called *Finding God*, by Dr Larry Crabbe and its words left indelible impressions on my heart as I fought to remain faithful towards the Lord.

Everything in me wanted to give up on God again, like I had, aged 17, when my foster sister was murdered, and my best friend died of cancer. I wanted to accuse Him of failing me, even of hating me, but this time I chose to believe the Scriptures instead.

God will have us revisit the same mountain again and again, so we can make different choices this time around and solidify a whole new mindset that replaces the old.

This is how He literally renews our mind, with brand-new neural pathways forming in place of the old.

The first round of chemo had a terrible effect on my son, but for your sake, I will spare you the details of what he went through and what I saw as his body was overwhelmed by such powerful and harmful drugs. It was truly shocking and disgusting.

When the consultants entered the room after that first round of chemo, the atmosphere was dark and depressing.

Their faces told the story, and with great sadness, they began to explain. "We are really sorry, Jay. We have some very disappointing news. Ordinarily, we would expect the cancer to shrink significantly after this first round of chemo, normally seeing an up to 50% reduction in size, but we've got the MRI scans back, and it only appears to have decreased by 11%. We can only hope that the second round does more than it normally does, which is usually another 25% decrease, with the last two finishing it off."

I was trying to take it in. What were they saying? That, in *our* case, the chemo isn't working?! *What is going on, Lord?! Why aren't you helping me?!* I inwardly yelled.

Fighting hard not to give in to the mocking voice of the enemy, I forlornly relayed the news to family and friends.

It took a while to process everything, but I became aware that the anger that was beginning to rage inside of me could either be channelled towards God or towards our true enemy... Satan.

The Lord kept speaking to me through God-incidences and dreams that, 'This Is WAR!' And I decided in my heart that I was not going to give up my son's life.

Over and over, I read about the importance of faith. Unswerving faith. The kind where significant obstacles are removed as the Scriptures promise: '...whoever says to this mountain, 'Be removed and be cast into the sea,' and does not doubt in his heart, but believes that those things he says will be done, he will have whatever he says.' (Mark 11:23)

The Lord was teaching me the power of my words and of speaking Life. In Jeremiah 1:10, Jeremiah spoke of the calling he had been given by God - from before his physical birth – to use his prophetic gift to bring about sweeping change: "See, I have this day set you over the nations and over the kingdoms, to root out and to pull down, to destroy and to throw down, to build and to plant."

He would do this with words. Solomon, with his supernatural wisdom, understood the power of our words, too. He wrote:

"Death and life are in the power of the tongue, and those who love it will eat its fruit." (Proverbs 18:21)

I understood from the Lord that this time, I was going to war with my mouth rather than my fists. I was going to tear down the work of the enemy with the prophetic Word of God. Paul taught this same principle to Timothy when he wrote:

"Timothy, my son, I am giving you this command in keeping with the prophecies once made about you, so that by recalling them you may fight the battle well..." (1 Timothy 1:18 NIV)

Strangely, it was also around this time that the Lord began to speak to me about 'going full circle', which meant I was going to start again.

In an incredible sequence of events, too detailed to share in this book, I found myself leaving the church I had been an integral part of for 6 years - and being led back to the very church that my family had helped start thirty years earlier.

In fact, my own battle for my son's life reminded me of the one our Apostle and his wife had fought over their own son decades earlier. Their son had been diagnosed with stage 4 cancer, which had spread throughout his body.

I learned that the Apostle and his wife received a prophetic Word from Psalm 118:17 for their son and declared it over him, over and over again: "*He* shall not die, but live, and declare the works of the Lord." In the end, he was miraculously healed.

So, I found myself back in their congregation, and they joined me in prayer for my son. It was as if the Lord said, "Jay will need someone who has been there before, someone who can support him in faith."

Again, as I began attending my new church, I fasted for 40 days and called on everyone I knew, in our old church and in this new church, to pray with me as we went to war. I began to speak Life over my son as he slept, to declare that he would be healed and fully recover. To prophesy that he would be a father one day and that God had plans for his life.

I even began to hear the Lord speaking to me about the Prophet Elisha and his battle to save the widow's son:

'Then Elisha got on the bed and lay on the boy, mouth to mouth, eye to eye, and hand to hand. As he stretched himself out over him, the boy's body became warm.' (2 Kings 4:34 BSB)

So, during the night after the next stage of chemo was carried out and before the scans were done, as a prophetic act, I acted out something similar as a symbol of faith, and spoke life into his body and cursed the cancer within him.

It seems the Lord loves it when we act out prophetic Words for Him. He did this often with Prophets in both the Old and New Testaments, and He still does it today. Agabus acted out a prophetic Word with Paul's belt:

"When he had come to us, he took Paul's belt, bound his own hands and feet, and said, "Thus says the Holy Spirit, 'So shall the Jews at Jerusalem bind the man who owns this belt, and deliver him into the hands of the Gentiles.'" (Acts 21:11)

The next day, when the Consultants came in, they were beaming with joy and incredulity: "We have great news!" They nearly shouted.

"We're not sure what's happened, it's certainly unusual, because we would normally hope for a 75% reduction overall by now... But your son's cancer has actually reduced by 89% overall, so now there's only 11% left."

A total reversal! Before, it had only reduced by 11%. Now, only 11% remained.

I responded to the small group of consultants and medical students who surrounded us: "Well, I know what's happened, the Lord has healed him! We've been praying and fasting for him, and God has responded!"

They replied, "Well, whatever it is, it's great news and *touch wood*, the last two bouts of chemo will destroy the rest of it."

I countered them immediately in what must have sounded oh so super-spiritual: "I'm not 'touching wood', unless it's the wood of the cross! It's God who is going to heal him."

Now this may have sounded very trite, contrary and unnecessary, but I was learning at that time how easily we as Christians can naively accept the statements, proclamations and by default false prophecies of others over our lives and those of people we know.

Not willing to build up expectations, doctors will prophesy the worst-case scenario, but rather than 'receive their report', like the ten spies who came back with a negative report, we need to declare, with faith, what God is going to do in any given situation, just as Joshua and Caleb did.

Our Words are *immensely* powerful. They create - either *good* or *bad*. Prophets need to steward their Words more than most. We can get into agreement with the devil and prophesy death over situations, or we can speak the very Words of Jesus, who described Himself as the *Resurrection and the Life*.

Chapter 4 - Reflections:

Point 1: Prophets *cannot* compromise. We need to die to self and choose to put God first in every area of our lives. We must *never* stray from or contradict the Bible.

Point 2: As we step out in faith and prophesy detailed and specific prophetic Words, the Lord will give us more. If we are *faithful with a little*, He will give us more responsibility.

Point 3: Prophets must learn to speak Life. Even if we see an apparently hopeless situation, we must not receive the report of the enemy or the natural realm. Instead, we need to ask the Lord for what future He sees, and we declare Life instead of Death.

Chapter 5: The Change

In fact, it was not long after my son was completely healed from cancer that I was having God-incidences about name changes again. This time, I had begun to believe the Lord was asking me personally to leave behind the season of mourning I had been in regarding my foster sister and best friend. I knew I needed to enter into a new season.

Rachel, when she was dying, called her son 'Ben-Oni', which meant 'son of my sorrows', but Jacob changed his son's name to 'Benjamin', which means 'Son of my right hand'. Jacob wanted to declare the favour of God over his son, rather than commemorate death and sadness.

The Lord was highlighting to me that as I spoke my son's name over him, I was affirming death and keeping old, sad memories alive, and He was asking me to change his name and to declare a different name over him that would speak Life...

As I mused about this, I began to pray, "Lord, if I try to change his name, the rest of the family won't agree. He probably wouldn't want to change it either, so why are you bringing it up?"

The following day, my son came home from school and declared, "I want to change my name, *I don't like what it means...*"

I was stunned, and I placated him a bit, thinking this couldn't be necessary and that the family would give me so much grief. But a few weeks later, it was the school holidays, and as we drove to our church camp, I asked over my shoulder: "So son, how are you feeling about your name now?"

"I still want to change it." He replied immediately. "I want to go by my other middle name, Nathan."

I was genuinely surprised that after several weeks, he had maintained his position on it, so I said: "Look, the rest of the family probably won't agree, but if God confirms it's His will, I will do it. Let's pray that God will speak to us about it, at camp."

So, we prayed and left it at that. Half an hour later, as we drove onto the site where all the tents were being set up, I inwardly prayed: "Lord, I'm going to need some help putting up this four-person tent. The boys won't be big enough to do it."

And then I found our area, and a young lad from church came straight up to my car before I could even get out, and asked:

"Do you need a hand with your tent, Jay?"

"Definitely!" I responded, "How has your morning been?" And then, he and God answered our earlier prayers:

"Actually, it's been pretty eventful. I was at the Deed Poll office this morning, ... I've officially changed my name!"

"Whaaaaat?!" I said. "I had no idea. What led you to do that, mate?" I asked, aware that the Lord was speaking.

"Well, my name had negative associations, so I decided to change it, and I'm using my middle name now instead...."

I could not believe what I was hearing, and yes, I felt God had set the timing of that situation up to confirm His will for my son.

God *OFTEN* speaks through timing.

Something 'just happens' to occur on the same day we have prayed about it. We overhear a conversation about something that has been on our mind. We happen to bump into the very person we have been considering contacting.

So, from then on, I began to declare "Nathan" over my son, which means 'Gift of God'. Everyone at church adopted this name change, too, which was amazing - and that cancer never returned to this day, and never will.

A few months later, I was up praying on One Tree Hill, as was my routine, and I felt so saddened that so many family members had not supported this decision and that my son was now called by one name at his mum's place and in that circle of people and "Nate or Nathan" at ours.

I asked the Lord: "Is this really ok, calling him two different names like this, Lord? Is it going to affect him negatively, or will it be ok?"

A few minutes later, I got into my car to drive home and switched on our UK Christian radio station, and immediately I heard the preacher say:

"Most of you would know me as Stuart Briscoe, but in actual fact, for half my life I'm known as David. In the business world, I'm David, and in ministry, I'm Stuart, and that's ok!" He went on to preach a great sermon and later wrote:

'When I worked in the bank, if you asked for Stuart Briscoe, nobody even knew who that was. I was Dave Briscoe in the bank. You ask in the church, I was Stuart Briscoe.' (Heroes of the Faith) - I just thanked the Lord for confirming that things would be ok.

It was also in 2007 that the Lord finally answered my cry for help regarding the development of my prophetic Gift. I had been recording my dreams for nearly 7 years by this point, sharing the literal ones but struggling to fully understand the symbolism and stories in most of the literal-symbolic or symbolic dreams I was having.

Then one glorious day, my father let me know that a friend of his had a son called David, who was also a Prophet, and he had recently advertised a *Prophecy, Dreams and Interpretation* conference which would be taking place at their church, not far away from us, in just a few weeks' time.

I signed up immediately, and wow, it felt incredible to flow in the Spirit and to hear so many of the same symbols in my dreams unpicked and explained. I learnt so much about the source, context, parables, wordplay, parallels, repetition, and the possibilities of dreams and visions.

One night, while on the course, I had a dream in which I was driving a car at 56.4mph. The interpretation I received from David came from Psalm 56, verse 4, which reads: "In God, whose word I praise— in God I trust and am not afraid. What can mere mortals do to me?"

At the time, I was fearful that our boys' custody would not be split evenly, so I was reassured to know that, as *I kept travelling* with the Lord in this mode of trust, it would not be 'man' who decided the situation, but God. Sure enough, custody was split fairly 50/50, to my great relief.

After the conference, David offered to stay in contact with me personally, and I'm pretty sure he regretted it once I began inundating him with dreams to interpret. Still, he generously blessed me with his time and energy, and during that time of mentorship, something really 'clicked' for me. I found that, like Joseph, I too could interpret dreams.

The Lord began to teach me how to really 'hear' and 'see' the point of the dream. I put this down to my heart posture. So, since 2007, I have interpreted literally thousands of dreams for myself and hundreds of others.

Eventually, in 2012, I established an additional Christian Dream Interpreter Facebook profile on which I have interpreted many, many dreams for several hundred people from all around the world. I continue to do so, but I have to protect my time, so I only respond once a week.

Just like my now friend David, who was himself mentored by a Prophet called Hany Soryal, who was mentored by Prophet Rick Joyner and Prophet John Paul Jackson, I was demonstrating a heart of humility and submission, the prerequisites to significant spiritual growth. As such, the Lord gifted me more.

After the *Prophecy Dreams and Visions* conference, I was asked to become a youth worker at the same church where it had been held, and I really enjoyed that role for six months.

Although I was grateful they prayed with me for my son to be healed, I wasn't at all impressed with my own church. It seemed dull and lifeless. I began to wonder if the church where I was now serving as a youth leader on Friday nights might be better for me... There were younger folks around, and you know, I might want to find a wife...

So, one Sunday, I decided to make my excuses and attend their church instead of my own, and afterwards I thought I should receive prayer and a prophetic Word from some of their folks—people who didn't know me or have any vested interest in my life.

The urge to leave my current church and do something new and exciting had become incredibly strong, and because I had left one church not that long ago, it now just seemed easier to consider leaving another.

After that Sunday service, I asked for some prophetic input, and so an older guy and two ladies stood around me and listened to the Lord for a while as I inwardly prayed: "Can I leave, please, Lord, and come here? I really like these people. This is a really great church, and I reckon I would fit in well here."

My plea was interrupted as the older guy began to speak. "I believe you've been wanting to leave your old church and find a better place, but the Lord is asking you to stay where you are and trust Him, and if you do, He will bless you there..."

Man, I was so annoyed. This was the exact opposite of what I wanted to hear. On my way home, I complained to the Lord: "When am I going to get something good, Lord? Why do I have to stay in such a boring church?" But as we'll see by the end of this chapter, I'd soon learn why hanging in there can be so important.

Prophets have to learn to give up the leading of their lives to the Lord and to trust wholeheartedly in His direction, because only God knows what He has lined up for us.

So, despite the crushing feeling of heading towards a divorce and losing access to half of my sons' lives, and feeling 'trapped' in a not very exciting church scenario, the idea of being mentored and developing my prophetic gifting was still exciting.

I could smell the faint scent of hope and could relate to Job, who, in his despair, wrote:

"For there is hope for a tree, if it is cut down, that it will sprout again, and that its tender shoots will not cease. Though its root may grow old in the earth, and its stump may die in the ground, yet at the scent of water it will bud and bring forth branches like a plant." (Job 14:7-9).

By the end of 2007, I had accepted that I was to stay in my new (*old*) church, and I was now emailing David, my mentor, regularly, and all of that was good. But the only problem I had now was the fact that the boys' mum had officially filed for divorce, and any day soon, that envelope would come through our letterbox.

As I waited for the bad news and accepted the loss of any faint hope of reconciliation I might have still been hanging onto, I developed a type of fear, called 'dread', which I would have to deal with later.

The divorce Decree Nisi eventually arrived, and then became Absolute in December 2007.

It was during this awful period of waiting that I woke up from a dream in the middle of the night and heard the Lord say very clearly, *"Stop working and seek Me for three months."*

Now, I would never normally condone this kind of decision-making and would counsel others only to quit one source of income if God has already lined up the next one, but when I asked, "How can I do that?! I would need £3000 in savings or something." The Lord replied as a thought in my mind: *"See what you're owed."*

So, I got my notepad out on the bedroom floor in the middle of the night and began adding up which courier and man-and-van jobs I had not yet been paid for, and the total came to £2200. I was pretty impressed. "Ok, Lord, what about the other £800?" I prayed.

The next day, I dropped the boys off at school and bumped into another father from church who almost immediately asked me, "Hey Jay, have you applied for that additional parent funding the council is giving out right now? You would probably get it." And yes, it was £800 in total.

So, as I turned 30, I began to pray and fast for those three months, seeking God's comfort, His plan for my life, and even for ministry. It was actually in 2008 that I moved back into the very same apartment I had lived in 7 years earlier, number 30A. Although it was hard to accept, I really had 'come full circle' and was starting again.

Chapter 5 - Reflections:

Point 1: Prophets will experience 'death' in many ways as we change, if you like, from a caterpillar to a butterfly. Friendships die as we become more and more passionate and sold out for Jesus. Family relationships sour as the devil provokes loved ones to turn on and reject us. Significant attacks on us, or our immediate family, force us to face death square in the face and *go to war*, or to give up and lose.

Point 2: Prophets must learn to endure misunderstandings and cope with the judgment of those who believe they have it all together. Jesus will ask us to pick up our cross and follow Him, for He too was: "...despised and rejected by men, a Man of sorrows and acquainted with grief. And we hid, as it were, *our* faces from Him; He was despised, and we did not esteem Him." (Isaiah 53:3)

Point 3: Crushing can be good. Olives are crushed to release oil. Grapes are crushed to produce wine. Prophets will face a crushing of their egos, their hearts, and their aspirations. We have to learn to trust our Heavenly Father to lead our lives, even if it means starting over.

Chapter 6: The Coaching

Despite those three months of prayer and fasting, going into 2008, I had become restless. I just wanted to have some consistent income, a job that made me look good, especially after only working part-time during my son's ordeal with cancer, and well, this just seemed perfectly reasonable to me.

So, even though I knew I hadn't fully submitted my will to God's will yet, or even heard His plan, I applied for a job I had no peace about, and got it.

In Feb 2008, I became a Youth Worker and Teacher in a Pupil Referral Unit (PRU) and for a year 'enjoyed' a mixed role of project management, mentoring young people and teaching life skills.

As I did so, I began to develop a love for teaching, which would prove significant later. Sadly, the job I had taken was a detour that came along, just when the Lord wanted to call me further into ministry. Not every open door is from the Lord.

Prophets must learn to genuinely test the spirits and confirm that what they are hearing is from the Spirit of God, not a deceiving spirit.

As I had prayed, I had been asking the Lord for a 'Green Light' and then told myself I was willing to see a 'Red Light' if it wasn't God's will. In reality, I was only looking for that *green* light, and so, guess what, that's what came up. I was then stuck in that job until the end of that year, as I dreamed of 'missing the boat' and other scenarios that made it clear I was now taking a detour.

As we seek to receive Words, Visions, and Dreams from the Lord, we need the same discipline to discern the proper interpretation of the message God is communicating.

All Words, Dreams and Visions can have multiple meanings or applications, and people mistakenly try to interpret God's Words using Bible-based symbols, dictionaries, and their own intuition.

However, as Joseph or Daniel would say, the actual interpretations belong to the Lord, and He shares those with whom He chooses.

Generally, God will not force His message on us, especially if we are not really listening. He will even allow us to go on detours.

During this year, I was learning to 'Let Go and Let God'- a lesson that would be repeated many times over the next decade or so. The Lord will only entrust interpretations to those who diligently seek His will and who give up any desire to twist things and manipulate the outcome.

Everyone has a gift, but not everyone is willing to die to self and allow the Lord to develop it and use it to its full extent, for others. I decided I would rather die to self and learn to kill off my flesh than repeat endless cycles of detours and mistakes. We all have that choice to make.

As I continued to be mentored by David and looked for more input from Godly peers at church, I began to realise how all Prophets need mentors, or in today's vernacular, *Coaches*.

In Samuel's day, he had a poor example in his mentor, Eli, who failed to discipline his own sons. However, it may well have been Samuel who initiated his own school of the Prophets to help those up-and-coming Prophets develop their gifts.

Interestingly, when those young Prophets saw Saul, the future king, prophesying, they wondered if he was one too:

"So, it was, when he had turned his back to go from Samuel, that God gave him another heart; and all those signs came to pass that day. When they came to the hill, there was a group of prophets to meet him; then the Spirit of God came upon him, and he prophesied among them. And it happened, when all who knew him formerly saw that he indeed prophesied among the prophets, that the people said to one another, "What is this that has come upon the son of Kish? Is Saul also among the prophets?" Then a man from there answered and said, "But who is their father?" Therefore, it became a proverb: "Is Saul also among the prophets?" And when he had finished prophesying, he went to the high place." (1 Samuel 10:9-13)

Prophesying doesn't make you a Prophet. The Spirit *came upon* multiple people in the Bible, who were not Prophets, and yet they prophesied. Even Caiaphas prophesied: "It is expedient that one man should die for the people..." John 11:50

Likewise, since Pentecost, anyone can prophesy through the gift of prophecy, but not everyone is a Prophet.

Later in 1 Samuel 19, we read: "And when they saw the group of prophets prophesying, and Samuel standing as leader over them, the Spirit of God came upon the messengers of Saul, and they also prophesied."

So, Samuel was called. Mentored to some extent by Eli, then Samuel mentored multiple others in their gifting as Prophets.

The young Prophets must have wondered from the interactions between Samuel and Saul whether Samuel was also mentoring Saul as a prophet; but in fact, in his role as a Prophet, Samuel was anointing and preparing Saul to be king.

Prophets anoint *kings* and teach other Prophets to anoint *kings* too: "Elisha the prophet called one of the sons of the prophets and said to him, 'Gird up your loins...go to Ramoth-Gilead and anoint Jehu king of Israel.'" (2 Kings 9)

It is part of our role to reveal the call of God on the lives of others. An International Prophet I really respect just recently prophesied that a man he knew nothing about would actually become King in his country, and that's precisely what happened. *Kings* or *Queens* can be leaders, or people of influence. They will either love us and seek us out, or seek to kill us off.

In 1 Kings 18, Obadiah hid one hundred Prophets to protect them from being slaughtered like the rest of the Prophets, as Queen Jezebel sought to silence God's voice in the land. Prophets need protection. Jezebel's desire to silence God's voice through the Prophets is surely a sign to us all that any desire to silence Prophets is demonic in origin.

In fact, in Matthew 23, Jesus said: "Therefore I am sending you prophets and sages and teachers. Some of them you will kill and crucify; others you will flog in your synagogues and pursue from town to town." And this same murderous spirit is alive and well in today's church. Still seeking to silence the Prophets. Prophets that Jesus Himself is sending.

Matthew 23 is all about the demonic religious spirit behind the Pharisees, who, time and time again, murder the Prophets.

In 2 Kings 2, the Prophet Elisha, who was being mentored by the Prophet Elijah, was approached by two separate schools or groups of Prophets, some from Bethel and some from Jericho. Both groups had agreed that the Lord was saying Elijah would soon be taken away: "Now the sons of the prophets who were at Jericho came to Elisha and said to him, 'Do you know that the Lord will take away your master from over you today?"

There were high numbers of Prophets in this setting, presumably because they were being mentored and taught in 'schools' how to discern the Lord's voice accurately. In 2 Kings 4, we see them living and growing together.

In 2 Kings 6:1-2, we read: "And the sons of the prophets said to Elisha, 'See now, the place where we dwell with you is too small for us. Please, let us go to the Jordan, and let every man take a beam from there, and let us make there a place where we may dwell." Their school was too small; there were so many of them.

In the Old Testament, they used terms like 'sons' of the Prophets and 'Father'; for example, when Elisha called Elijah 'Father', even though they were not blood relatives. (2 Kings 2:12)

Having said that, there are also two Prophets who are understood to be the son and grandson of other Prophets, and I certainly believe God calls and gifts a family line, not just individuals. My own son and daughter are already accurately prophesying in our church setting.

Zechariah was actually the grandson of Iddo the Prophet, as we see in the book of Zechariah, but quite intentionally listed as the 'son' of Iddo in Ezra 5:1-2: "Then the prophet Haggai and Zechariah the son of Iddo, prophets, prophesied to the Jews who were in Judah and Jerusalem, in the name of the God of Israel, who was over them. So, Zerubbabel, the son of Shealtiel and Jeshua, the son of Jozadak, rose up and began to build the house of God, which is in Jerusalem; and the prophets of God were with them, helping them." We see here that prophets help build, both literally *and* spiritually.

The Prophet Hosea was the son of Beeri, who, according to the Talmud, was also a Prophet: "There were forty-eight prophets and seven prophetesses who prophesied to Israel... Among them was Beeri. Because he prophesied only a few verses, his words were included in the Book of Isaiah." (Talmud, Megillah 14a)

Clearly, Prophets need to be fathered and mentored as they grow in character and discernment, as I was privileged to experience, spending a year or so under David's mentorship. He took the time to invest in me as I became a prolific dreamer and began to hear the Lord in ever-increasing ways.

While all this purifying and growth was happening, I was having incredibly accurate dreams, even dreaming sixteen dreams in one night, and I was aware that this was not the norm for most.

A little way into 2008, while much of Christendom was being wowed by a prominent Evangelist, the Lord showed me in a dream that this minister had fallen into sin and needed to be stood down. This happened later, in August of that year.

So, the Lord again revealed to me something of international significance to the whole Body of Christ, and I felt humbled that He would entrust me with such a revelation.

So many Christians dismiss the voice of the Lord as He tries to correct their behaviour or choices, perhaps directing them to dress more modestly, or to mind their speech, to reduce physical contact, or to rebuke someone else who is clearly in sin.

As soon as they feel challenged by the Spirit in some way, they begin justifying themselves, looking around and arguing: "Well, so and so does it, and they seem to be doing ok." This hardening of hearts leads to a lack of discernment. Believers who should have the mind of Christ, mindlessly follow the next fad, and chase after the next spiritual superhero. The Word says, "Where there is no revelation, the people cast off restraint." (Proverbs 29:18)

The biblical response to any minister who is behaving in an ungodly manner is to rebuke and correct their behaviour, not ignore it or justify it.

When we see any Christian brother or sister living sinfully, we are meant to 'go and tell him his fault between you and him alone (Matthew 18:15) and to "restore such a one in a spirit of gentleness"

(Galatians 6:1). The Bible is our authority; the world's standards are not. In today's church, this doesn't seem to happen much anymore.

Right now, around the world, there are countless 'Christian' leaders being exposed, and yet in many cases, thousands of *'sheep'* still flock to their services. It is incredible how far we have fallen from the days when there was a genuine fear of the Lord present. This is the kind of capitulation to Jezebel that the Lord refers to in Revelation 2.

It is very easy to be misled, even as we ask God to confirm His will for our lives. We put out fleeces, never thinking to include one that says 'no'. Our problem, as Jeremiah put it in chapter 17 of his book, is that "The heart is deceitful above all things".

We can see warning signs in a person's behaviour, in their character, in a ministry that relentlessly asks us to 'sow a seed' or an opportunity that we want to take, but have no peace about, and still go ahead, dismissing the lack of peace we have, hoping it will all be ok in the end.

I actually discovered that my friend had applied for the same job I started at the beginning of 2008, and when I got it instead of him, this drove a wedge between us. Not only that, but I often had to literally run to work from the train station and back, as dropping my boys off at school and catching the train was extremely tight, time-wise.

Although this Christian organisation was great, the people were wonderful and my role pretty fulfilling, I felt like Jonah, needing a whale to come and grab me, so I could be puked up on the beach and head back to Nineveh.

As I said earlier, if we want something badly enough, we will 'see' the signs and confirmations we want to see, and God will often sit back and allow us to crash through the wrong thing for a while, before we are genuinely ready to listen to His plans and obey His voice.

This is why, as the Bible teaches, we *must* seek outside input (preferably from Prophets), especially when making life-changing decisions.

And we *MUST* make sure the guidance we receive lines up with the Scriptures. If we are seeking to leave a church, we need to ask ourselves, "Why am I so eager to go somewhere else? Have I truly served where I am? Do I have a good heart towards those I 'do church' with? Have I become proud, thinking I am superior to these folks in some way? And most importantly of all — Is God *actually* calling me somewhere else to fill a gap in the body of Christ, or am I needed where I am?

So often, especially among younger folk, believers do not heed the Bible and serve where they are needed, even though God's way is to place people where He wants them: "But now God has set the members, each one of them, in the body just as He pleased." (1 Corinthians 12:18)

Instead, many young people want to be where things are *happening!* They want to end up on stage and make a name for themselves, but all the while, they are simply chasing the bright lights of selfish ambition.

As we saw in my own story, it is God who places us in a church body, so before moving, we need to be *VERY* sure He is placing us somewhere else, a place where we are *needed*, or where we need to be. Otherwise, we need to stay where we are and build that church.

As a Pastor now, I see this repeatedly — people become bored, look for a new buzz, and move from one thing to another, whether it's a job, friendship, relationship, or church, all the while claiming that God is leading them.

Mostly, He is not. They are leading themselves. They have either become offended, fallen into sin, and want to hide in another church, or they are struggling to submit to the leadership of the church where God deliberately placed them.

As the Lord reiterated to me in this season, our flesh needs to be made subject to our spirit, and we need to give up living for ourselves and for our own glory and start living for His. (Romans 8)

By November 2008, I could no longer tolerate my job, so I handed in my resignation, feeling frustrated by my tendency to try to fix things in my own strength and angry that I had delayed God's plans instead of waiting on Him in faith.

In January 2009, I began writing my first book, and the experience was incredibly cathartic. I realised as I wrote that book and tried to wait on the Lord that He would provide for me in His own ways, and I had to learn to make decisions that made God look good,rather than me. I would argue that a Prophet has to *die to self* on a whole other level, because sometimes we will appear foolish, doing things that others, in their worldly wisdom, will sneer at.

Frequently, Prophets prophesy something 5 or 10 years in advance, and as those prophecies have not yet occurred, people start to doubt us.

We can sometimes come across as overly passionate or 'emotional' because we actually feel the Lord's grief when we share a Word or air our concerns when we see someone or something being exalted or given authority, even though we know they should not be trusted at this point.

And sometimes the Lord might ask us to prophesy something, only to then relent from the original prophecy due to repentance or concerted prayer, and now we look stupid – Jonah complained about that scenario.

The key is to obey and to leave the rest up to the Lord. In the end, He will vindicate us, whether now on earth or in heaven.

The *heroes of faith*, some of whom were Prophets, understood this reality. "All these people were still living by faith when they died. They did not receive the things promised; they only saw them and welcomed them from a distance, admitting that they were foreigners and strangers on earth." (Hebrews 11:13 NIV)

Anyone appraising Isaiah, Micah, or Daniel would have very quickly concluded they were false prophets. After a year or so, a decade or two, and then a century or two, their prophecies about the Messiah coming, even from Bethlehem, looked a little, shall we say, 'desperate'.

So, the life of a Prophet is oftentimes pretty challenging. We hear from the Lord, then, like David or Jonah, we rail against the Lord and want to know why He is taking so long to act or not acting at all! Or like Isaiah, we prophecy something in advance, not sure we will ever get to see its fulfilment.

In a more subdued place now, I got on with writing that book. But even as I did, I struggled with my pride and angrily prayed, "I used to be top of my class, Lord! I've got a Bachelor of Science degree with Honours in Product Design! And here I am writing a silly little book that no one will want to read. And even worse, I'm claiming *housing benefits!*"

I felt so humiliated. *Housing benefit payments are for poor people,* I thought, as I battled with my ego.

In fact, there came a day when I couldn't take it any longer, and I literally went to the Social Security office to tell them I didn't need their money and that I would be fine without it...

But God, who is Sovereign, did not want me to miss out on all that provision, and He began to bring up the story of Elijah at the brook Terebinth, highlighting that it was 'unclean' birds that brought him his provision in that season.

In obedience, I repented and returned to the social services office (the equivalent of Centrelink in Australia) and asked whether it was too late to stop them from cancelling my claim. Thankfully, it wasn't.

I was genuinely embarrassed, but in the end, the Lord was right. In fact, I saved thousands of dollars during that season, which I would need later on, as you will see.

So, I continued to write that first book, and I was also invited to design a commercial website for a church friend and earned some money that way, too, but a visitor to my house had prophesied 'the best was yet to come', and sure enough, God had it all in hand. My future was about to get a lot more exciting and enjoyable.

In the summer of 2009, I played a key role in bringing Prophet John Paul Jackson over to the UK to minister at one of our church camps. He was, if you like, a hero of mine, mainly because he had taught on Prophecy, Dreams, and Visions for such a long time, with proven integrity, wisdom, and a record of being highly accurate. I felt I could absolutely trust the Words the Lord gave this man.

In the months leading up to his one-night visit to our church camp, the Lord was speaking to me about the story of Lazarus and the prophecy in Joel 2, which declared God would *"restore the years the cankerworm (locust) had taken away."*

Sat with my boys and my mother in the big tent as he finished his impactful sermon, I turned and said, "I've got to go and speak to John Paul. I need to know if I am really hearing from the Lord."

My mother could see my desperation and told me to go, so I rushed through the rows of chairs just in time to meet him before he climbed into the car parked next to the tent and headed off to the airport.

"Excuse me, John Paul," I began, "I'm sorry to bother you, but could you please pray for me?"

By this point, my youngest, Elijah, had caught up with me, wanting to see what all the fuss was about.

"Sure, I can!" John Paul said with a magnanimous smile and kind eyes. He offered to prophesy over my son as well.

Now I won't share my son's prophecy with you, but I can tell you it was indeed accurate, and I have done my best to respond to the Lord's direction over the last fifteen years. I will, however, share the exact words of John Paul's prophecy over me:

Without delay, he prophesied: "Thank you, Lord, that you are going to raise the dead in this man's life, like Lazarus! I thank you, Lord, that you are going to give him back all the years that the cankerworm has taken away!" And he finished prophesying.

He had literally just repeated back to me the exact two prophetic Words I felt the Lord had been declaring over my life for the previous few months. It was wonderful.

The Prophets are indeed subject to the Prophets. (1 Corinthians 14:32) And as Paul records the principle in 2 Corinthians 13:1, "In the mouth of two or three witnesses shall every word be established."

In those next few months, I was invited to join the Leadership and Theology training program of our church movement, and as previously explained, someone felt led to pay my fees.

So, in September 2009, I began one of the most enjoyable academic years of my life. On reflection, I realised that if I hadn't detoured into that other one-year job I took in 2008, I could have started a year earlier... but thankfully, our God 'brings good out of bad, for those who love Him'. (Romans 8:28)

At one point in 2009, as I regularly visited my parents' place and walked to Noah's Ark, I began to have several God-incidences about the story of Noah's Ark. As I was still fasting and praying and dying to self, I wondered if God was trying to say something to me, or about me. As I walked into my flat and prayed out loud:

"Lord, I feel like maybe you are asking me to build an ark, Lord, like Noah... You keep bringing up that story, so what is the ark Lord? What am I building?!"

As I was talking, I turned on the TV. The channel I had left it on from the night before was the *God Channel*, and a well-known Prophet appeared on screen, and the words he was speaking at that exact moment, as the sound came on, were: "Some of you are building an ark. And you don't know what it is. But sometimes this is what He does, God gets us to build an ark, and the ark is our soul!" I was utterly stunned. What a precise and clear answer from God!

The ark was my soul! *Well, that fits!* I thought excitedly. *I've been preparing for what you have for me, and I've been fasting and praying so that I'm ready for a new start. Noah had to start again, too.* Little did I know that this 'season of Noah' would unfold in much more detail and carry a much more profound message.

So, I finished writing my book called '220' – which was all about the battle to die to self and live for Christ, to kill off the ego and independent mindset and truly submit to the Lord as Paul taught us in Galatians 2:20 – and I also got stuck into serving and learning from some very gifted teachers on the Leadership and Theology course I had enrolled on.

It was incredible; I loved every minute, and the Lord continued to shape my heart and coach me into a place of submission and trust.

On one occasion, as we were placed at different churches 'on mission', another student and I visited a young lady who had been suffering with stomach pains for quite some time.

As we prayed, I felt led to declare the following prophecy: "For there is nothing hidden that will not be disclosed," which was Luke

8:17 and then continued: "Lord, I prophesy that you will 'bring to the surface' exactly what the issue is for this young lady. You will reveal what needs to be done to heal her body, in Jesus' Name!"

That night, I dreamt one of the most unique dreams I have ever had, in which I was lying down, and my appendix was trying to push itself out of my stomach. As I woke up, I literally grabbed at my stomach to try and stop it 'bursting' through the surface of my skin and then realised it was 'just a dream', even though I could still feel the sensation of the organ pushing out through my stomach.

My appendix was *'coming to the surface'*.

That day, the young lady I had prophesied over, was taken into the hospital and her appendix was removed in what was apparently life-saving surgery, as her appendix was about to 'burst'!

I continued to minister over those few weeks of local mission and away in Turkey in a much more challenging environment. Still, every opportunity to lead people to the Lord, to preach and to minister the gifts of the Holy Spirit was incredible.

After 6 years of living as a single parent with an independent mindset, I was learning to trust and work with people again. Also, I had been keeping myself pure and allowing the Lord to renew my mind, and according to the Lord, the 'ark' was ready...

Enter Noah's wife!

Chapter 6 - Reflections:

Point 1: Every Prophet needs a 'Father' or Mentor in the faith. There is a season of service and of humbling ourselves that we all need to go through. This breaking makes way for maximum growth and for a more fruitful use of our gift.

Point 2: God will 'raise the dead' in our own lives, removing the strongholds of fear or rejection, hurt, betrayal and all the rest - as we deepen our personal relationship with Jesus. *Dying to self* allows us to 'come alive' to Christ.

Point 3: Sanctification takes time. Remember that all Prophets in the Bible had long delays, detours and their own wilderness experiences. Nothing has changed. God doesn't change. He still works the same way.

Chapter 7: The Covenant

We actually met on Valentine's Day 2010, as I was halfway through my academic year of study, which in the UK would end in June and July, and it was on this day of romance that this pretty, laid-back Australian lady called Dee arrived at the Training Centre where all my studies took place.

She had been offered a role as the childrens' worker in my own church congregation (the one I was going to leave) and would live in the flat on the first floor of the Training Centre, where I would spend most days for the foreseeable future.

We got along well from the first night we met, and within a few months, we were spending a lot of time together building a great friendship. My year of training went brilliantly, and I graduated with distinction in July 2010 and with a firm desire to serve the Lord in ministry for the rest of my life.

When summer arrived, I was offered a part-time job as 'Housekeeper' at the Training Centre and was assigned a role on the team to help train the following year's cohort. At our church camp that summer, I was also invited to teach on Dreams & Visions. This was such an enjoyable experience for me, and the feedback was fantastic.

Dee and I worked together for the remainder of the school summer holidays on an outreach program to primary-aged children. When we got into the early part of the first semester for the new cohort, Dee had to fly back to Australia for a few days to her friend's wedding.

It was at this point that God 'lifted the veil' and we both realised we loved each other. After some cryptic conversations over the phone, I met her at Arrivals in Heathrow, and we shared a kiss that should have been in a movie!

It wasn't long before we discovered that she had family from 'Rainbow' in Australia, and with mine at the edge of 'Noah's Ark', it definitely felt like God was bringing us together. In fact, we discovered that she had lived around the corner from me as early as my first year at university. If I had only waited and not gone with the first woman to show interest at that point in my life, I could have married Dee ten or more years earlier.

So many young people, like me, make life-changing decisions that nullify, divert or delay God's plans coming into being. As I now teach often regarding decision-making, we all need to slow down and: "Never make a decision if we feel flushed (with emotion or passion) or rushed (pressured into something by someone else's will or timing)."

In the summer of 2011, two very significant things happened. Firstly, Dee and I felt the Lord calling us to church-planting, and in our own context, could not see how that could happen.

Although we had tried to stay in submission at our church, we had begun to feel as if we were being 'heavily shepherded,' and the Lord gave me a dream in which he was 'helicoptering' other people and us out of our congregation.

Unbeknownst to us, several other couples were sensing the Lord leading them to new callings, too.

In fact, I had a dream about one of the key guys - our church Lead Pastor - in which the Lord clearly spoke to me about His plan for this man's life.

In the dream, I arrived at our leader's house, and they were moving. There were boxes everywhere, so I called out: 'Wow, looks like you guys are moving. Would you like a hand? So, I started shifting boxes and bags. Suddenly, I became aware that his oldest son was standing at a window, preparing to jump. I realised it was my job to catch him, so I urged him to go for it and caught this older lad in my arms.

As I sought the Lord for the interpretation the next day, it came quickly. So, I rang this dear man and shared the prophetic Word.

"Hi," I said. "I had a dream about you, which I believe is a prophetic Word. Are you happy for me to share it with you?"

"Sure, Jay, go for it." Came his response.

So, I explained the dream the Lord had given me:

"Ok, well, the Lord showed me that you guys are on the move, you are moving. He also showed me that you have a gift (the older son), which I know nothing about. In the dream, you had an older son, which I know you don't have in real life, but our children often represent our gifts. So, this son was about to take a leap of faith, and it was my job to catch him. This means I need to let you know that you have a gift I don't know about in real life, which is actually quite mature (meaning well-developed), and God is saying, 'If you will take a leap of faith with this gift, He will catch you.' Does that make any sense to you?"

He was shocked and excited to respond: "Yes, it does, Jay. I have been doing photography for a long time as a hobby, and I've been feeling like God might want me to pursue it as a career."

Within a few short months, he and his family left the church, moved a fair distance away, and joined a local church. Incredibly, he secured a photography contract with a restaurant chain with venues across the UK, and later became the principal photographer and vlogger for a large clothing chain. This was the favour of God on his life as he obeyed the call.

All the couples who left did so independently of one another, and I was assured that God was guiding a group of us towards better things as we obeyed His voice.

So, in our situation, as we prayed and fasted, asking the Lord to explain precisely how He would use us in a church-planting context, we had no idea what God was about to do.

At the end of that fast, Dee received a message from a Senior Pastor in the church movement she used to belong to, and which we are now part of, asking: "Would Dee and her husband-to-be be willing to plant a church for us in the UK?"

We felt this had to be the Lord. Soon after, we informed our leadership and discovered that the other couples were leaving at the same time, just as the Lord had shown me.

While I believe we are to stay wherever God places us, I also believe God will shift some people out to give them a fresh start, or He will shift some disruptive people out to give the remaining people a fresh start.

In this instance, we felt the Lord was calling us and these other humble and gifted couples to come under new leadership, so that He could fulfil His plans for our lives.

It is also critical to note, as I teach in seminars on Prophecy, that couples will eventually BOTH hear God on everything. Joseph and Mary both heard God's will regarding the parenting of Jesus.

In a relationship, the Prophet may hear God first, but there will be a peace for the spouse; later, there should be confirmation, leading to complete agreement. God will confirm His will if we are both truly listening, as He views married couples as *one*.

Prophets who have not *trained their senses* will jump from one church to another, from one town to another, dragging their poor spouse around with them, because they are not submitting to Scripture or the leadership of others. We *MUST* test the spirits and check our hearts, and our spouses will need the chance to review our decision-making or prophecies further down the line. Always get a second opinion and two or three witnesses.

We thought God was saying He wanted to use us to plant a church. Our then leadership did not agree, but God wanted us to join another Church movement, and He caused our Senior leader to reach out at the exact right moment to confirm it was God's plan.

The second significant event that occurred that summer was that Dee and I got married on 6th August 2011!

We had the most beautiful wedding and chose the Rainbow as our wedding theme. We were fortunate to secure the license for Norman Adam's *Rainbow* painting from the Tate Gallery, which we used throughout our wedding stationery. God's prophetic statement to Noah in Genesis 9:3, "Now I give you everything", became one of the two prophetic Scriptures over our marriage.

In the build-up to our wedding, we were blessed in many ways, and in the end, we found we had only £567 left to pay off all our wedding costs. One final incredible wedding gift came in from a lovely couple we consider to be really good friends, who contacted us to let us know, "God gave us a very specific gift amount that we should give you, so we hope it makes sense to you when you see it on your bank statement." You guessed it, they gave us the exact amount... £567!

Remember how God had given me a heart for teaching back in 2008? Well, he had given me a dream back in the Spring of 2011, and it was exactly accurate. The dream depicted me looking for and securing a dual role (which turned out to mean: studying and teaching at the same time), and it was at my old secondary school.

There was an urgency in the dream to seize the opportunity before it disappeared, so I woke up knowing I needed to explore ways to study and teach, and to act quickly before someone else took the last space.

The Lord opened the door for me, and sure enough, my old school wanted a Design and Technology Graduate teacher, *and* there was *one* fully funded place left on the university's initial teacher training programme when I applied, which I got.

So, the month after getting married, Dee got a fantastic job in my sons' Christian primary school, and I began a Graduate Teacher Program at the school I used to attend as a kid, and I began teaching my beloved subject: Design and Technology. Our interviews were on the same weekend, and we were both successful.

The Lord had suddenly begun to bless our lives. In fact, I had a dream about being in the house Dee used to live in years before (I had never been there), and when we enquired with her old landlady about whether that house or any others were available, we were told it was just becoming available and that we could have it with no bond!

This was a bona fide miracle in London and an answer to a specific prayer I had been praying just prior: "Lord, when we get married and move into our own place together, I want us to begin our new life with no debt, to have a brand-new start together."

At the time, Dee had some significant debts due to her frequent back-and-forth life between the UK and Australia, so we sold her old car, used my savings, which I mentioned earlier, and then used my £850 bond to clear them completely.

By October 2011, we were ready to move into our new home, just as I had asked the Lord: happily married, debt-free, and extremely excited about all that the Lord was going to do as we planned to plant a church for Him soon, somewhere locally in London.

What followed was a season of coaching of a different kind, as our Senior Pastors came over from Australia several times and supported us as we prepared to start a church for our movement.

In 2012, my wife, who is also a Prophet, had an incredibly accurate dream that went as follows: 'A young girl arrived at our front door and had a sorrowful expression on her face. Her father stood somberly next to her and said, "There are things twisting in her intestines, and she can't absorb the nutrients from food" She also saw a twisting helix.'

Upon waking, my wife told me this dream, and I interpreted it, "The girl in your dream has the same name as the baby we know that has just been born. It is about her." (That family had cancelled plans to come for dinner the previous evening, telling us the hospital was keeping their daughter in, as she might have an infection) – "We need to pray for her right now, Dee." I continued, "She is seriously ill."

Only a short while later, we received the news that the baby girl did indeed have a twisted bowel and was unable to absorb nutrients, precisely as the Lord told Dee in her dream. As we prayed, the doctors were trying to save her life.

Now, because we had received this warning in a dream, we concluded that the Lord wanted to see this little girl not only saved but healed, so we began fasting and praying as we would in any serious situation, praying our hearts out for a miracle.

Surgeons removed all the twisted intestines, but then had to tell the parents that her bowel was too short to be reattached and that she would be on Total Parenteral Nutrition (TPN) for whatever life she had. But we prayed that her intestine would grow, and it did!

Our friend, her mum, called us to explain that they had found a blockage at the tip of the intestine, where it was cut, and now, it had mysteriously started to grow! We kept praying that it would reach the 2 cm needed for reattachment, and it did.

So, the surgeon reattached the intestine, and despite her parents being told she would never eat real food, God worked miracles to such an extent that she now eats normally.

Apart from the occasional spiritual drama here and there, over the next 5 years, we actually had a season of 'doing church' in our home, as we saved up our tithes and had babies - four in fact – and the Lord gave each one a prophetic name.

The first, 'Samuel', was given his name as it kept coming up for us, and when old friends invited us over for dinner and wanted to share a prophetic word, they told us, "Not sure if you've settled on a name yet for your baby, but we really feel it should be 'Samuel'."

In 2013, Dee was pregnant with our second child, and we had discussed calling him Joseph, even though we had already picked 'Joseph' as one of Samuel's middle names.

One day at work, as she wrestled with the idea, God used a little 'prophet' named Benjamin to confirm his will. As she walked down the corridor, Dee remembers praying inwardly: *Lord, is it too weird to call our second son by one of the middle names of our first son?*

And then her train of thought was suddenly interrupted by this little boy she occasionally taught when she covered another class:

"Hi, Mrs Reynolds, what are you going to call your baby?" Dee responded: "'I'm not sure, Benjamin, what do you think we should call him?"

Benjamin replied, "You should call him the name of an important person in the Bible."

"I agree," said Dee, "Which name do you think would be right?"

"I think you should call him 'Joseph!'"

Our Sophia (which means 'wisdom' in Greek) was given her name through God-incidences, which were then confirmed when one of the staff at Dee's pregnancy scan came to assist us, and her name was *Sophia*.

'Daniel' was named in like manner, with multiple confirmations of his name and one of his middle names reflected the season we were entering into at the time.

After leaving the church movement I had been part of my whole life, we realised we had a lot to process. As I 'climbed the ladder' in my school setting, life became very busy with four under-fives and my older sons living with us half the week. So, we kept things 'in-house', literally, with just a few additions to our family 'doing church' together.

We needed to learn a lot about pastoring, which came through many interactions with our senior leaders and the couple from Australia who had been led to plant a church up in the North of England.

As I grew in my role as a teacher, I also honed my preaching and teaching skills within our church community. However, internally I was battling that fear I mentioned earlier, which haunted me in many forms: dread, fear of failure, fear of rejection, and fear of inadequacy.

Elijah the Prophet had this same battle. On the outside, he was full of confidence and accurate in His Prophecies, but inwardly, he was fragile. Often, a bullish, even aggressive exterior can hide a fragile, insecure interior. In this next season of life, however, the Lord was going to force me to face and overcome my fears. There was no getting away from it.

Chapter 7 - Reflections:

Point 1: God is committed to us, just as He covenanted with Noah. Even if the whole world seems to be against us, we can rest assured Jesus is *FOR* us!

Point 2: God will confirm His will for our lives through multiple witnesses. We need to be willing to fast, pray, and ask for clear leading and Godly Counsel *before* making big decisions.

Point 3: Sometimes, God will move us on, especially if He needs to discipline leadership and correct ungodly behaviour in those who mistreat us. Our challenge will always be to keep a pure heart and to bless those that curse us.

Chapter 8: The cave

Prophets can be tempted to operate in isolation. The rejection, the stifling control of others, and the fear of missing the mark can cause Prophets to 'give up' and go into hiding. As a result, many Prophets around the world are not in subjection to any leadership at all and operate as lone rangers, often becoming lone wolves.

Not being in submission to a church body can indicate a wounded heart or a rebellious spirit, and those who isolate may harbour resentment or pride. As a result, they become the mouthpiece of the enemy rather than of God.

To be *in Christ* is to be connected to, to be a vital part of, and to be submitted to: His *Body*, after all: "Christ is also the head of the church, which is his body.' (Colossians 1:18 NLT)

Part of baptism is being baptised *into* the Church body. "For by one Spirit we were all baptised into one body." (1 Corinthians 12:13)

As we declare with our mouths that Jesus is Lord over our lives, we are affirming our submission to His Government and leadership from that moment onward. We are becoming citizens of His Kingdom, and His Government is His Church.

Yet plenty of people *attend* a church, and they are not, as the Apostle John put it, 'part of us'. They claim to be Christians, but they will not be led by Christ in the way He wills, *through His Church*.

If we are doing our own thing, we are in rebellion against Jesus' own body, just the same as cancer cells rebel against the human body.

So, the 'Cave' can be a dangerous place. We can get there through burnout, betrayal and heartache, sin and depression, or, as in my case, fear and insecurity. People go off the rails when they reach this 'place' and begin to seek something 'new', in the demonic *winds* of doctrines, *earth-shaking* conspiracies, or *strange* fire.

However, God is still found in the stillness, in His whisper. He is the Unchanging Constant, rather than the 'New' and counterfeit, just as Elijah the Prophet learned when he arrived in his cave.

We must be careful not to 'chase after the wind' when we end up in a cave season, otherwise we will inadvertently or even intentionally end up in the *New Age*, seeking something exciting that the Lord actually detests.

The Church is still God's answer. His Word in the Bible will *NEVER* be replaced, and He will restore us if we hang onto Him and outlast the attack of the enemy.

As we reached the early months of 2013, with no formal church yet established, I felt increasingly inadequate as a Pastor and simply unable to start a proper 'church'. Consequently, I poured all my energy into my work, hoping the pressure to establish an official church would disappear.

Instead, as I excelled in my work environment and became a Head of Year, the pressure to start a church was replaced by the pressure to keep 208 students on track in an inner-city school in London. This role led to a lot more stress and significantly less hair!

I was paid well and had some status at our school, but I also faced significant opposition from what I can only call *Jezebel* spirits.

I'm not going to explain this phenomenon in full at this point, but essentially, as any Prophet steps forward and begins to use their gift healthily, they put themselves on the front line of the spiritual battle.

It has certainly been my experience, and that of many other Prophets worldwide, that, like Elijah the Prophet, we keep coming up against 'Jezebel'-spirited people. 'She' immediately reacts to the mantle on us. If you remember, this is how Elijah came to be in the 'Cave'.

When we use the term *Jezebel,* we are referring to people, sometimes leaders, who only want to get their own way. They will do whatever it takes to maintain control over us, and the situation, whether it's coercion, manipulation, intimidation or forming alliances against us. They are full of pride and ego and resist the Spirit in us.

This might be the boss who takes a dislike to you, despite minimal interactions. Or the peer who seems flirtatious despite knowing you are married or that they are. As long as you toe the line, they flatter you, seem very open with you, and even sensual, but as soon as they realise you don't need their approval or have no intention of compromising your faith, relationship, or anything else, they turn against you. This happened to me in several different settings, and it was pretty challenging to handle.

Prophets tend to be very up front. They often wear their hearts on their sleeves. As they prize integrity so highly, they seek to be authentic, sometimes expressing their true feelings too freely and at the inappropriate moment and often giving themselves to people who are only half as interested in the relationship as they are.

Although I tried to keep my head down at work, I felt the intimidation, control and constant monitoring from a couple of senior figures and peers who had this *Jezebellic* mindset.

This happened in both of the schools I worked at. You don't have to be a Prophet to know what kind of people I am talking about.

They are controlling, two-faced and manipulative. They will flash smiles at you while plotting your downfall. They use you and take from you while planning their own rise to power over you.

Fortunately, as with every workplace I've been in, I had the ear of the head of the organisation in both of these schools.

Prophets often find themselves in this position. Peers may turn against them, line managers might oppose everything we stand for, but frequently, God aligns us with the 'king' of the setting we're in.

This allowed me to succeed and influence the curriculum in the schools where I worked, despite genuine opposition, while upholding my integrity regarding the content we were pressured to teach. During this period, I learned, like Daniel, to maintain my integrity while adapting to the pressures of living under Babylon's influence.

In 2014, the extremely below-market-value rent we had been paying on our place in Greenwich was about to increase to a level we couldn't afford. So, we started asking the Lord where He would have us live.

One crazy day, two separate people said, "You should live in Shooters Hill." And another said, "I've heard Shooters Hill is a great place to live," And so we began looking for a house in that area, which happens to be the third-highest point in London. This was the Lord leading us to exactly where He wanted us.

As we began browsing through the many options online, I had the crazy idea that I'd really love a big, open-plan living space, so large that we could play table tennis indoors! (This was because of our brilliant British weather) Despite our limited budget, my wife also believed that we needed two bathrooms.

So, we began praying to the Lord for a place with those particular features. This is another example of how the Lord guides us. He provides us with a specific desire, which helps us eliminate all the wrong options and narrows them down to the one He has for us.

We gave notice on our old place, and once again, the Lord began to bless us. Our Landlady bought our washing machine from us at full market value for a brand-new one and then reduced our rent by several hundred pounds in the last month, just to help us as we moved. We felt the Lord genuinely wanted us to see this as His way of guiding us up to Shooters Hill.

Over the next few weeks, I had been experiencing God-incidences, regarding the passage about Jesus preparing a 'mansion' for us (John 14), so I felt as though God had something lined up.

But with just one week left to move, as you might expect, we were feeling pretty worried that our answered prayers wouldn't arrive in time.

Then one night, as we drove to pray outside a place that had literally just come onto the market, we stopped at a train line and waited as the train passed by.

As the gate swung open, I inwardly heard the Lord say, 'I'm opening up your place for you.'

The next day, as we officially viewed our future home at Rosekey 'Mansions', we discovered it had a huge lounge downstairs (easily big enough to play table tennis in), two bathrooms, and a yard that wasn't even included in the description. We felt the Lord had led us to our new home. With just one day remaining, we moved into our new place, high up on Shooters Hill.

I believe the 'high place' is significant. Abraham took Isaac up there. Moses went up there often, with two others holding his arms as he oversaw the battle from that vantage point. Elijah went up there often and defeated the demonic opposition of the prophets of Baal up on the 'high place'. In fact, Jesus *frequently* withdrew up there.

So, life went on for a couple of years as we got used to living high up above London and enjoyed the stunning views from Shooters Hill. We had baby after baby, ending up with four under-fives in the end, and having young children helped us settle into our new community.

Meanwhile, very significant questions were being asked on the international stage, and the Lord wanted to share His heart on it all.

On June 22nd, 2016, I asked the Lord how He felt about the British referendum, which was about to take place the following day. The vote was to decide whether the UK would remain part of the European Union or leave it.

During the week before, I began to ask the Lord about His thoughts on 'freedom'. As I prayed that night, the Lord led me to read a book called 'Out of Control', which I had never read before and which had been sitting on my bookshelf for several years.

I 'accidentally' opened it on the page titled: "Freedom", so I assumed the Lord was about to speak to me. As I read on, the author discussed the secularism that had taken hold of the UK after it joined Europe and ultimately the European Union.

It described the gradual removal of God from our nation, and as I read it, I was in total agreement, feeling sorrowful about our unfaithfulness as a country and also bemused that this content was even in that book.

Now I could go on about how I felt God was emphasising these words to me, but instead I want to take the opportunity to explain how Prophets constantly need to operate in faith.

When we ask a specific question and get a specific answer, as I did, by picking up the book and opening it on the correct page, we need to choose by faith to believe that this is God speaking. This is 'child-like' faith, the kind that Jesus loves. He *led* me to that book and page.

It is exceedingly rare for anyone to hear God's voice audibly. I believe I have heard Him that way, only once. The rest of the time, we are left with two options: we can believe God is speaking through extraordinary 'coincidences', accurate dreams or visions that turn out to be true, follow urges or unctions to speak or act, that lead to miraculous and confirming events, and believe they are God's will...

Or we can dismiss these occurrences altogether and chuckle to ourselves about how absurd it is to believe God Himself would speak to us personally. But Jesus made it very clear in Scripture, first, that all believers should 'know and recognise His voice' (John 10) and, second, that we must have faith if we want to please Him.

God is not impressed by our academic achievements, slick presentations, or stoic, business-like leadership. He is pleased when we act in faith—believing we have heard His voice, been moved by His will and emotions about a situation, and obeyed that voice and instruction. Just reread Hebrews 11 if you don't believe me.

When I picked up that book, I had also been hearing the word 'Equilibrium' over and over. It had been swirling around my mind for the previous week. As a result, I posted online that I felt God wanted to bring about Equilibrium through this referendum and shared excerpts from that book explaining why we, as a nation, needed to exit the EU (Brexit). This was a prophetic Word.

So many Christians are carnal. They only ever use their natural senses and never venture into having 'ears to hear' as Jesus put it.

In their pride, they really believe they '*Know* What Jesus Would Do', about any and every situation, but oftentimes the Truth about *WWJD* is that Jesus will do what He can, and *only* when believers listen and obey. Very often, He does not do anything on the earth because He cannot find a willing vessel.

Imagine how much closer we would be to seeing Jesus come in His Glory if more believers understood what God wanted from their lives and did exactly what He called them to do, in complete submission to His will...! Isaiah said, 'Send me!', but most Christians are saying: 'Send someone else, and I'll give them a 'like', or I might even share their posts as a show of support!'

Jesus refuses to operate outside of us. Paul tells us why: "For we are *God's fellow workers,*" (1 Corinthians 3:9). Jesus wants to work *with* us and *through* us, not in spite of us.

We have a relational God who is keen to share His heart with us, as His individual disciples, and with us as His church body through His Prophets.

Very often, we assume we *know* what Jesus would want for our church, as we plan our next outreach or teaching series. Pastors even look at other churches and think, "Well, they're growing, let's imitate them, forgetting that God works in unique ways in each different setting.

It is tragic that so many churches are oblivious to God's heart or will for their local area and proudly claim they are 'doing the Lord's work', when they've actually never taken the time to listen to Him or to invite Prophets to speak into the matter. They might not be doing the *Lord's* work at all.

If you ask a Pastor or Apostle: "What is the Lord saying specifically to you right now about Australia? Victoria? New South Wales, South Australia? Melbourne? Sydney? Adelaide? The state, town or city that you are in?" Would they have an answer to give? Most likely, they will provide a generic all-encompassing response like: 'Well, you know, we need to fulfil the Great Commission'. Or, 'God hates the sin in the world, He wants us to shine like lights in the darkness'.

Statements that anyone, even unbelievers, could quote from the Bible, but those are all just the *'Logos'* (written) Word of God.

Romans 10 tells us that faith comes from the *Rhema* Word of God. When prophetic words reveal the hidden content of an unbeliever's heart, as in 1 Corinthians 14:25, the person prophesying is not merely quoting Scripture. Jesus is speaking through that person about the world we live in and the circumstances, or heart of that specific person they are prophesying over.

God has specific things to say to every church, too. Just recently, our own church received a *Rhema* Word from Ezekiel 37. 5 years ago, that Word would not have made any sense to us, but now it does. We have also heard the Lord challenge us about our lack of prayer, and, like the vinedresser in John 15, we are pruning off all unproductive branches to focus on praying for Revival.

Unless you have received a prophetic Word regarding your church and had it confirmed, how could you know what Jesus wants to do in and through your individual church, town, or area?

Jesus has specific things to say to each of our individual churches, as modelled in Revelation 2 and 3.

All too often, Apostles, Pastors, and Teachers assume our role is simply to plant churches, nurture them, and teach the Word.

But Jesus also promised us that *the harvest is plentiful*. So, we should ask ourselves: 'Are we witnessing a great harvest yet? If not, why not?'

Peter and the others fished all night on their own, then, suddenly, Jesus told them to lower their nets again in a specific place, and, in response to the *Rhema* Word of God, they caught a huge haul.

I recently challenged a bunch of Pastors who represented a number of churches in a couple of different nearby regions, by asking:

"Is all our outreach *actually* working? How many people have we seen saved in the last 5 years?" The numbers reported were depressingly low.

That question is, of course, quite confronting for Pastors, especially those of us who have felt the pressure 'to perform' and 'be successful'. It's also important to recognise that in the Western World, we can start to believe that having a 'decent' church with a few salvations and baptisms here and there means we're ticking along nicely.

We should be asking ourselves more profound questions, like: *Are we experiencing revival? Are hundreds and thousands of people getting saved? Or is the influx of new people simply due to church transfer? Are itching ears seeking a better experience at a cooler, younger, slicker church with better coffee?*

We need to hear God's perspective on everything and not settle for the comfort zone. And once we hear His Voice, we need to respond accordingly.

As decreed by the Lord and prophesied, Britain eventually left the EU in 2020 and has recently begun to experience revival.

This worked example proves how desperately we need to understand the overarching principle that Paul taught: "...we do not wrestle against flesh and blood, but against principalities, against powers, against the rulers of the darkness of this age, against spiritual hosts of wickedness in the heavenly places." (Ephesians 6:12)

The Lord revealed to me that Brexit was necessary to free Britain from the grip of the principality of secularism, and now we can understand why: because there are clear signs of Revival in the UK as church attendance is on the increase and UK celebrities are giving their lives to Jesus. Something had to change for that to be possible.

The Old Testament teaches on this subject in the book of Daniel, and we would do well to realise that every town, city or area has its own principalities and powers that we are, in a sense, 'under'.

In our town, the principalities or powers are witchcraft, rebellion, intimidation (bullying is prevalent) and greed.

In another town, it might be violence, robbery or perversion. Either way, we need a revelation of precisely what we are up against and of God's strategy to resist and displace our enemy.

So, how do we make sure we are hearing God's voice and not our own? How can we be *sure*?

All Prophets need to learn this lesson, so they can prophesy accurately and prevent any of their flesh from creeping in to sway or misapply God's Word.

Dee and our family had been visiting Australia since we got married. After enjoying our second 'honeymoon' there in 2011, we had been back together as a family a further three times.

Overall, we had felt for quite a while that we would end up living there, so in 2016, as we seemed to be going there every two years, 2012, 2014 and then 2016, we decided to ask the Lord if it was His will for us to move to Australia in 2 years' time; in 2018. And the Lord answered us in three distinct ways.

Firstly, while we were there in 2016, I was sitting with my senior pastor and coach in his car, waiting for him to finish a phone call.

Inwardly, I prayed, "So, Lord, are we coming here soon? 2018 maybe?" At which point, my senior pastor responded to the person on the other end of the line: "It's just a bit premature."

Even though I didn't want to hear it and couldn't wait to live in a sunny climate, those words stuck with me... "It's just a bit premature." God will speak this way, through timing. Prompting us to ask a question, just as He orchestrates the answer.

The Holy Spirit does the same when we read our Bibles: a verse or word sticks out to us, and seems weighty and important, just when we need to hear it.

But as we went back to school in September 2016, we were still asking the Lord whether we would move to Australia at some point, hoping I had misheard the 'premature' thing and that it would still be 2018. The Lord was ready to speak again on the matter.

We had been praying over those few months, and the story of my old childhood friend kept 'coming up'. He had been left behind in the UK while his parents pursued what they felt was the call of God on their lives and moved to another country. He was only a teenager at the time, and I knew how deeply it had affected him.

So, knowing that the younger of my two older sons would only be 16 by 2018, I knew in my heart this could not be right, even as my heart longed to move.

And this is part of the journey. We have to learn to recognise when we are being driven by our own heart's desire or by a desire God has put in us (Psalm 37). Even if it is God's plan, we need to submit ourselves to His timing in everything, rather than our own.

Very often, we rush to make things happen *way* before God's perfect timing, and when we do, it results in a lot of fallout, disruption, and hurt. The important lesson is this: The *Rhema* Word of God NEVER contradicts the *Logos* Word of God (the Bible), but God's Timing is just as crucial.

If God says, "Anyone who does not take care of his own household is worse than an unbeliever," then we cannot conclude that He is giving us the 'green light' to go off and do our own thing, leaving any of our household behind.

Of course, at 18, our children become adults and everything changes, but until then, they are our top priority. So many people are urged by our culture to: *'Follow your heart!,'* but this is a worldly deception. The Bible teaches that the heart can be full of selfish desires.

So, with all that in mind, Dee and I decided we should pray into it some more and one day, on my way to work with my older sons in the car I put it out there to the Lord in prayer… genuinely willing to hear His honest reply.

As I drove, I asked my sons to get into agreement with me as we prayed, and I prayed out loud: "Ok Lord, if *You* really want us to move to Australia in 2 years, in 2018, please speak to us and confirm this is *Your* will, Lord, thank you. Amen."

The boys chimed in: "Amen!" And I immediately turned on our UK Christian radio station, just in time to hear:

"Some of you are saying 2 years, but I'm telling you it will not be 2 years!" We were dumbfounded!

The guy on the show was discussing Jeremiah 28 and paraphrasing it in his own words, but we had our answer.

So, after I relayed this to Dee, we accepted that the Lord had spoken and that the circumstances in the natural were not lining up as they should, and we changed our question slightly to: "Ok Lord, *when* do You want us to move?" And the number 2020 just started coming up over and over again…

I had shoulder surgery in late December 2016, and the bed opposite me was number 20, but the sign was triangular so that you could see the number *20* from both directions. All I could see was '2020'. As the team of nurses pushed my bed to the theatre, I became bitterly cold as there was no heating in the hospital corridor and a very kind nurse turned to me and said: "You would be better off living in a warmer climate!" – Not the normal thing you would say in those circumstances, and I have since wondered if she was an angel.

We also realised that the younger of my two older sons would turn 18 in 2020 and would be able to make his own decision if he wanted to move to Australia with us, so we put the idea on hold and decided to revisit it closer to 2020.

This is the challenge for all believers, but even more so for Prophets. When we are chosen to be a mouthpiece for God, to declare His Word at any given time or season, we cannot be glib or casual about it. We should have such a healthy Fear of the Lord that we dare not attempt to speak on His behalf without being sure we are hearing from Him.

It is undoubtedly true that we might still miss the timing, the exact interpretation, or the application, but our hearts need to be set on only speaking His Words, in His way and in His timing, not our own.

We should be desperate to get it right. Willing to keep asking for more details as we go. Determined to only prophecy *Truth*. I'll come back to this subject in our final chapter.

As I recovered from the shoulder operation, God began to speak to me about being like Gideon and how He wanted us to get on with starting a formal church.

In the early part of 2017, we were now meeting as a church downstairs in our large living area - or as some might call it, the 'basement' – when a prophetic Word came out which I received by email. It spoke about some of us being like Gideon, 'hiding down in our own basements', just like he hid in the winepress...'

This felt like the Lord rebuking me, so I responded by taking the considerable risk of actually starting a church in a public setting.

We began by choosing a name for the church and settled on *The Rock Community Church*. I started designing our logo and website, and we all began praying that the Lord would lead us.

As we began to formalise the church, our friends who had been joining us intermittently went in the opposite direction and couldn't support us. So, like Gideon, we were left with hardly anyone; in fact, we had no one other than our own family of five, soon to be six.

I was petrified that we would fail and look ridiculous, but I obeyed and advertised the new church anyway.

As there were no venues available on Sunday mornings, we had agreed to rent the Church of England hall at the top of the hill in the afternoons, and on that first Sunday, we ran our church service 'as a practice' with just the five of us!

Of course, we were tempted to die of embarrassment because no one had responded to our online advertisement, and we wanted to give up right then and there.

It was incredibly scary, but the Lord loves our raw faith, and he gave my wife a dream about an old English bus, the kind you can hop onto as it drives by.

She saw people jumping on board as we started moving, so we took this as a Word from the Lord.

The very next week, our first wonderful family arrived, and they remain good friends to this day. Over the next week or so, their friends, another beautiful family, began to come as well.

Then, as we stressed about not having a worship leader and having to use videos, a young lady who used to lead worship at my first church suddenly turned up with her children. It was fantastic; she was still just as talented as I remembered.

Then another family came, who we had known from another church setting, and a few others started coming as well. Somehow, God just started building a church from nothing.

Around that time, Dee and I began to believe the Lord was speaking about 'praying out ungodly leaders from their key positions' (both locally and nationally) and we understood that the Lord expects us to 'pray for our (often ungodly) local and national leaders' in broadly two ways: either that they will repent, or that they will move on, or be moved on, and that they are replaced with someone more righteous.

The story of Nehemiah kept coming up as well, and it became apparent to us in this season that there are 'Gatekeepers' in our societies that we need to be aware of. Jesus called a positive example of such a person a 'Man of Peace'. (Luke 10)

Oftentimes, on housing estates or in certain areas, there is one matriarch or patriarch that everyone listens to. If *they* are on board, then access is granted!

At the time, Nehemiah faced significant opposition from some of the ungodly people around him because he was reestablishing Jerusalem and the strength of God's people by building walls and gates around the city.

As we persevered in prayer, we eventually saw several political leaders in our national and local contexts removed, and we learnt in this season the importance of 'praying through', of being aware of the 'big picture', and of safeguarding our Christian faith politically.

Recently, I prophesied that the Lord wants His people to rise up and take pivotal roles across our nation and internationally. We must strengthen the Church in our country by supporting key Christian voices in positions of influence.

The life of a Prophet is incredibly costly, often spent in the hidden place of intercession, praying God's will into being on the earth—whether locally, nationally, or internationally. We don't often get the limelight; we listen and obey, and most of the time we have to pray with passion, like Elijah did, for God's Word to be fulfilled on the earth. God is always searching for intercessors. He speaks through us, but He also works through us.

If God wants to say something to the whole world, He looks for someone to speak through. I'll repeat that earlier example: "Then I heard the voice of the Lord saying, "Whom shall I send? And who will go for us?" And I said, "Here am I. Send me!" Isaiah 6:8.

By relocating us to the top of that hill and helping us start our little church, and by beginning to speak about Nehemiah's challenges, God was starting to say something that would only later become apparent to our broader church movement and to the Church Universal.

The great thing about our God is that He continues to use the seemingly small, weak or insignificant to speak on His behalf.

If we are not careful in the modern Western Church, we might look for impressive people who are popular or powerful in some sense, and, like the Pharisees, completely miss *our day of visitation*.

The Lord chooses to send important announcements through 'lesser vessels', who are perhaps not as polished or remarkable. "...God chose the foolish things of the world to shame the wise; God chose the weak things of the world to shame the strong." (1 Corinthians 1:27)

While exiled in the desert, Moses 'turned aside', to a burning bush and ended up speaking with God face to face. Balaam received his rebuke through a speaking donkey, which perceived the spiritual reality of the angel before them, long before Balaam did. Mary and Joseph received The Word Himself, in total obscurity and were judged and rejected by many, despite carrying the actual Word of God in Mary's womb. Paul had a vision of a Macedonian man and completely changed the course of his mission, based on what might be considered a 'weak' revelation.

As hinted at earlier, Elijah the Prophet had to learn this exact lesson himself, when he desperately wanted to hear from the Lord: "...a great and powerful wind tore the mountains apart and shattered the rocks before the Lord, but the Lord was not in the wind. After the wind, there was an earthquake, but the Lord was not in the earthquake. After the earthquake came a fire, but the Lord was not in the fire. And after the fire came a gentle whisper." (1 Kings 19:11-12)

God refused to speak in an impressive, earth-shattering way. Instead, He insisted that Elijah should learn to respond to a whisper. I am on this exact journey myself right now, personally.

The point is that God will judge us for how we respond to the 'lesser' input that He chooses to give. He often said: "Whoever has ears, let them hear." (Matthew 13:9)

So, we need to be willing to 'listen' to whatever Jesus chooses to say, and through whichever means or vessel he decides to speak; even if it is a person or an occurrence that seems unimpressive.

Sometimes, though, God will speak, by doing something *extra*ordinary...

Chapter 8 - Reflections:

Point 1: Our hearts will deceive us. Our ego will cause us to isolate and 'do our own thing'. We need to be sure what 'spirit we are of' and only operate under the leadership of the Holy Spirit, not cursing people or situations, but rather blessing.

Point 2: God can speak in many different ways and through many different means. We need to be listening all the time. But we also need to be discerning. If *anything* we hear does not line up with Scripture, then it is *NOT* God.

Point 3: God just loves faith, and Prophets will need to grow in faith to use their gift in more impactful ways. We can take steps and 'test' a Word, without over-committing to a project or calling, but we also need to be willing to lay things down if they prove not to be the will of God.

Chapter 9: The Confirmation

Midway through 2018, we started praying about finding a new venue to meet on Sunday mornings instead of in the afternoon. We understood this would be tough, as there were very few actual venues in our area, and the school down the road, which I had contacted back in 2017, had outright refused, saying they had never rented it out and probably never would. But God was preparing an incredible sequence of events that would unfold over the next few years.

After moving into our new apartment directly opposite that school in May 2018, the school was taken over just a few months later, in August 2018. It consequently changed its official name to 'Ark' Greenwich Free School'...

As you might remember, the story of Noah was fundamental to me initially and then to us, as a couple, especially in relation to our marriage. So, the idea that our little church, now named "the Rock *Family* Church" - after the Lord prompted me to change it from *Community* to *Family* – could actually end up 'in the Ark', seemed just too God-incidental *not* to be God.

I told Dee excitedly on the phone: "Guess what? They've changed the name of the school across the road from us to... are you ready? 'Ark' Greenwich Free School,' And now we are the Rock 'Family' church, it would be like Noah and His 'Family' going into the Ark!"

She was equally stunned and agreed it had to be the Lord, so we told the church we intended to look into it and started praying hard.

When I rang the school in September 2018, I was surprised to discover that the premises manager shared the same name as someone I grew up with. Although it wasn't the same guy, I felt like something was being set up for us, and I eagerly rang to speak with him.

"Sorry, no", came his curt reply. "We've never rented it out and probably won't do so any time soon, but I can take your details in case anything changes?"

What a disappointment...

"Sure", I said and gave him my contact details. After that call, I prayed inwardly: *Lord, this has to be You. Why isn't the door opening?!*

But as is often the case with the prophetic, God reveals to us ahead of time what He wills, so that we can pray His will into being.

We often assume every Word is a 'now' Word, when in reality the Word is God's plan or desire for the future, and the journey to experiencing its fulfilment has only just begun.

Thankfully, we only had to wait a couple of months before the Lord started speaking to me about His *'Perfect Timing'*.

"Dee," I said, "The Lord is talking to me about His Perfect Timing. I'm going to ring the school again tomorrow." She was very used to this kind of conversation and agreed that this was probably a good idea.

The next day, as recess was ending at the school where I worked, I felt the urge to ring the school's premises manager: "Hi again, it's Jay." I began, "It's been a couple of months, so I'm just ringing to see if anything has changed...?"

"Your timing is UNBELIEVEABLE", the property manager gasped. "I can't believe that! I have LITERALLY just walked back into the office after being told that we ARE going to rent out the school from now on! Your timing is just incredible".

I confidently replied with a beaming smile on my face: "Well, I reckon it's God's timing. So, what do we need to do? Have we still got first refusal?"

"You have," he replied, then went on to explain that they would need to get an external company to value it and organise tenants.

A couple of months later, in January 2019, I was looking at the Ark organisation's website on the Saturday night before preaching at our friend's church, wondering why it was called *Ark* and asking the Lord to reassure me that this was definitely His plan. I was praying that the rental price, which was due to be decided by mid-January, would not exceed £150, as that was all we could afford.

The next morning, we travelled the short distance to our friends' church, and I was looking forward to bringing a Word on 'Coming Forth as Gold'.

We got there, and I recognised a few faces from the joint Men's Breakfasts we had run, and from years before, when we were part of the same church movement. Otherwise, we didn't really know anybody else.

As we stood up to sing during worship, I kept reflecting on the school's name, 'Ark', and what God was up to with the Noah story.

All of a sudden, their in-house Prophetess came up to the front and asked the leader if she could share a couple of Words.

She was invited to do so and immediately looked at me as the music continued playing quietly in the background and announced, "You are God's *NOAH*, aren't you?"

"I saw the name NOAH over your head, you are called to be God's NOAH!" She declared with great conviction.

I was astounded—genuine confirmation from someone who knew nothing of our background. I simply replied, "Yes, that's right," and enjoyed the moment as my family heard the confirmation and smiled happily with me. She then continued to prophesy some other encouraging Words over us as ministers.

Shortly afterwards, the property manager called to let me know the valuation was £150 and, incredibly, that the lease would start the very next week after our current lease for the hall at the Anglican church ended.

Although our lease started from April 7th, the other families were all away on Easter holidays, and we holidayed too, so we decided our first formal service 'in the Ark' would be Easter Sunday, April 21st 2019. That date would be *very* significant.

It was all very exciting at the beginning with a lovely hall and excellent facilities, but after a further six months in 'the Ark', our church wasn't growing, and the Ark-sized school hall that we met in remained largely empty.

So, as we neared the end of 2019 and still believing we were in our 'Nehemiah season', trying to build the Kingdom despite much opposition, we began to ask the Lord what He thought about us moving to Australia and in somewhat of a petulant act, began investigating buying a small apartment in Shooters Hill, given that it seemed unlikely the Lord was going to come through and shift us to the other side of the world, any time soon.

As we did, we felt no peace at all, and the Lord was letting us know He was not impressed by our actions. So again, we decided to take a day out to fast and pray.

We began praying: "Lord, please speak to us today about whether we are moving to Australia in 2020, or not? We need to know."

We also prayed, "Lord, if You want us to move, then it needs to be for another ministry position; we don't want just to move if there's no real purpose behind it... Otherwise, we will just put roots down here and forget about it." We continued to pray all day.

At 5pm that evening, my phone pinged with an email notification... A vacancy in our church movement had just been advertised.

As our church movement had started in Australia and spread from there, I realised it would most likely be a position in one of the 150-odd churches there. So, I opened the email...

"*DEE!!*" I yelled from the bedroom as I quickly read through the job advert. "Is there an *ARARAT* in Australia?!?"

"Oh yeah, there is," Came her reply as I found her in the kitchen. "It's not far from Ballarat."

"There's a job there, for Lead Pastor. They want someone like us."
"Imagine that," I continued, "like Noah, we go into 'the Ark', then we 'land' in *Ararat*, just like he landed on Mount Ararat! That would be crazy!"

We both felt this had to be the call of God on our lives and began to get excited that He was indeed relocating us to the other side of the world.

Now, as with all *Words from the Lord*, we are instructed to get a second and third witness, and if believers would only do that, a whole heap of heartache would be avoided.

So, apart from applying for the position, we resolved to seek out one or two respected and accurate Prophets to visit, so we could get outside direction from the Lord on what He wanted.

We knew of one accurate international Prophet based in the UK who had visited my old church many years ago, and of a younger Prophet who, on January 25th, 2019, prophesied that flooding would come to Matlock, Derby, in England— a very specific prophecy. This prophecy came true in November 2019, just as we were seeking someone who could accurately hear from the Lord.

As it happened, the more senior Prophet was mentoring him, and both were part of a church in Windsor, only an hour and a half away.

So, on December 29th, 2019, we decided to go just as a couple, leaving our children with supervision, and drove to Windsor in time for their evening meeting.

As we neared the church, our conversation returned to the confusion we felt about starting a church, only to potentially move out of the country a few years later. We discussed how we had thought we were in our 'Nehemiah season' and how it seemed strange to now be considering moving somewhere else.

We then agreed that the Prophet would need to clearly state we were moving *somewhere else* if that was indeed God's will.

Just before we arrived, I said to my wife: "You know, even though I've been listened to and basically all the prophecies I've shared have been proven accurate, I've still felt like a *Prophet without honour* here in the UK."

We discussed this for a few more minutes, then pulled into the venue and found a seat in the church.

The service was fantastic, and we were excited to hear prophetic Words being shared regarding 2020, but it was after the service that folks were invited to come forward and receive a personal prophetic Word from the senior Prophet of the house.

To put it mildly, this experience was mind-blowing. As we approached this little lady, we did not expect the pinpoint accuracy we were about to experience. We also didn't want to give anything away, so we just said, "We'd like to hear what the Lord is saying, please." And without hesitation, she just began to speak the Word of the Lord over us. These were her exact words, straight from the Lord:

"You *are* entering your Nehemiah season, which means you have to build. Says the Lord. And the Lord says, that you're not meant to be detoured from that. But I felt like the Spirit of the Lord says: We're still looking for the right place and the right location. And so, the Lord says: "Know this, I am in the process of transitioning you and giving you a different geographical place. And so, the Lord says: "Just because you know it's time to build, does not mean you build where you are. "Make the transition." Says the Lord. "And the Lord says: "And then He says, you'll see you'll have the manpower and the money power, " says the Lord," to even be able to build in those areas." Says the Lord. But also, I just want to speak: "Father, right now, where a Prophet is not recognised in his hometown. Father, we just declare that is not going to be what they take with them in the next season. Father, that there will be honour and recognition Father, in the Name of Jesus, Amen!"

This was truly incredible. It was as if she had been in the car with us on our way to their church.

To be recognised as a Prophet by another highly respected Prophet was beautiful and reassuring. But the accuracy of those Words from the Lord was also concrete enough for us to believe the Lord was indeed transitioning us out to the other side of the world, just as He had said, so many years previously.

As we stumbled towards the exit, in shock, we saw the up-and-coming Prophet we knew of standing near the back, so we stopped to ask if he would be willing to prophesy over us as well. He is now the most accurate Prophet I am aware of, so it was great we were able to get his input as well.

He began prophesying and declared that:

"The Lord has allowed you to hear some things that others might not be able to comprehend", that "God is going to use you like missionaries as your feet have been born to travel", and "The Spirit of God is going to release a missionary anointing on you." and finally, that "God has allowed you not to have unnecessary commitments."

He then shared God's heart: "I've got you used to 'sitting on the boat with me". And declared of our future: "You are not going to have to throw the fish back into the water". All of this was correct.

We had indeed '*heard some things that others might not be able to comprehend*' and were deeply concerned my older sons would not understand or be willing to relocate with us, and that our church movement and senior Pastors would not understand the need for us to leave the UK to walk out this prophecy and move to Australia.

In their minds, they had asked us to start a church for the movement in the UK, so why would God be moving us out?

But we also felt God had very specifically replaced us with a couple who came from Australia to the UK and started their church in the North of England before we even started ours, and, of course, as a Prophet, I had to trust my own ability to hear God's voice.

This Prophet had just confirmed we were going to be like missionaries in what, for our younger children and me, was a foreign country.

We had also moved into another rental rather than buying an apartment, and since this one was fully furnished, we had already sold a lot of our furniture. There had also been several relational disconnections, too, all of which meant, as he had prophesied, we had hardly any commitments keeping us in the UK.

I was consequently offered the position of Lead Pastor in Ararat just a couple of weeks later, and I gave my notice to the school I was working at in the UK, just in time to leave during the Easter holidays.

We were deeply concerned about how our leaving would impact the families in our church, but the Lord gave one of our key preachers two dreams over the Christmas break. The first one was the Lord saying, "You will need to find another church", and in the other dream, she was literally told, "Jay and Dee are moving to Australia".

Please note, we had not let on anything to anyone when the Lord spoke to her in this way through those two accurate dreams.

Our last service as a church and the last sermon I preached in the UK, was on Australia Day, January 26th, from James 5 and in it I prophesied for the first time: "The Rain Is Coming!" I believed then, and I believe even more now, that we are praying for and expecting the latter rains of Revival as the world comes to its end and Jesus returns for His Bride.

It was incredibly sad to accept we were leaving the UK and that it felt like we were as described in that second prophecy: *'throwing the fish back into the water'*, but as there were no replacement leaders, we felt we should recommend our church folks join our friend's church locally with us, for a few months at least, or look for another church home.

Even though it all seemed totally crazy, we were at peace that we had heard from the Lord.

Chapter 9 - Reflections:

Point 1: Delays can be caused by our own disobedience and pride; the attack of the devil who resists us, just as he did with Paul, or they might be down to God, who knows that if we are held up a bit, things will actually work out better in the end.

Point 2: We can and must get confirmation from other Prophets. There are various kinds of Prophets who 'see' or 'hear' in different ways – the key is to look for agreement. Our circumstances should align with the prophetic Word we declare or receive, but we might have to wait patiently for that to happen.

Point 3: Fear is like fog. All the moisture in that fog, that blocks, confuses and intimidates you, can actually fit into a normal-sized cup. We must make decisions from a place of faith in God, rather than from faith in the devil (fear), which comes from viewing challenges from the wrong perspective.

Chapter 10: The Completion

In January 2020, after looking at multiple flight options and prices to fly our family to Australia, I turned to my wife and said, "I really feel we should pray about which airline we should go with..."

"Ok, if you think that's important", came the reply, but I could tell she thought I was overthinking things.

As I have learned, though, Prophets need to go with their 'gut instinct', because more often than not, it's actually the Holy Spirit prompting us to take a particular course of action. "I think it's important, Dee, let's pray about it," I replied.

So, we prayed, and even though there were seven or eight options, several of which we had flown with and enjoyed, now, all I could think of was 'Qatar. Qatar. Qatar.' As in Qatar Airlines.

In my logical mind, I reasoned: "But Lord, Qatar is where those guys died, building the World Cup stadium. There wasn't much health and safety in place then. Why would we want to go with their Airline?" I couldn't see how they could be the right choice, so I read some reviews, and they seemed pretty good, and more importantly, the words just kept going around in my mind: 'Qatar. Qatar. Qatar.'

"Ok, Dee, I think we're meant to go with Qatar Airlines," I said.

"Ok, sure", came the nonplussed reply, and so I booked those tickets to fly out in April 2020, but as you will see later, this was a Spirit-led decision, and it really did matter which airline we chose.

It was around this time that the Lord gave me a dream about an 'ETA' and showed me exactly how I could apply for a spouse visa once I was 'on shore' (in the country). When I woke up, I looked up the details about an ETA visa, and sure enough, I found I could explore work opportunities while in the country on that visa.

I also discovered I could apply for a spouse visa once I was there and receive a bridging visa in the meantime, allowing me to work as soon as the 90-day ETA visa expired. This was fantastic news and meant I could go, knowing that when we arrived, it might not be the right place for us and we could come home, or that if it was right, we could stay permanently.

As you will all remember, those next few months, especially in the UK, were awful. COVID, the Alpha variant, spread at an alarming rate, and a friend of ours nearly died, another relative of a friend actually died, and several people we knew suffered lasting damage to their lungs.

Still, all teachers were expected to go to school and teach, and I vividly remember walking down the corridor, thinking, 'This is mad. Listen to that kid coughing his guts out as I'm walking past. What if we get the worst version and take it home to our family and friends?'

Soon afterwards, much to our relief, the schools went online for 'remote learning', and we continued to make plans to leave the UK.

The only problem was that international travel was rapidly grinding to a halt. Airline after airline cancelled all their flights to Australia and most other destinations, and all of a sudden, we got a call from our travel agent:

'All the flights are being cancelled up to Easter, could you and your family leave earlier, at the end of March maybe?'

'Sure, I said, I guess we'd have to. Will it cost anything extra?'
"Unfortunately, yes." She replied, "At this point, it will be an additional £1300..."

"£1300! I'm not sure we can afford that right now." I replied.

"Well, do you want to have a think about it and get back to me? Please be aware, there are very few seats left on most flights and all the airlines are restricting and cancelling flights altogether..."

I thanked her and took it to the Lord, feeling agitated that if I was indeed meant to leave my grown-up older sons in the UK at least temporarily, leave behind other friends and family and give up my home country, then He needed to make my path smooth, and not expect me to come up with more money for super expensive tickets!

"Lord, if we *are* meant to go, I don't see why it should suddenly be costing us a load more. Please confirm this is your will. I'm already giving up everything, Lord. I need you to sort this out, please."

Over the next few days, the story of Abraham kept coming up as I followed my own biblical advice and would not make a decision while 'flushed' by emotions like fear or panic or 'rushed', by the chance that seats would disappear.

Abraham had to leave his family and country, and God promised to bless his obedience. It felt as though the Lord was saying, "I will bless you, Jay, just like I did with Abraham, so just trust me and don't get despondent."

Roughly three days later, still trying to keep my cool and wait on the Lord for peace, I suddenly had it. I felt peaceful. So, even though I didn't want to use any of our savings, I rang up the travel agent and said: "Ok, we're happy to take those earlier flights."

"Mr Reynolds," came the reply, "I have great news for you! Because you waited, it turns out today falls within a cancellation or alteration period, which means the airline has to give you the flight at the same price as before. It's a good thing you waited! I'm sorry we hadn't realised this was being offered."

I was really relieved and thanked the Lord, but now we had even less time to prepare to move. In the end, we packed up everything in one week and gave away loads of our stuff for next to nothing. I had the distinct feeling, though, that God would return the blessings later as we obeyed His voice.

As I dropped off personal items and objects for my mother to store at her house and said my goodbyes, I literally had to hold my breath as I hugged her, just in case I was carrying COVID and could infect her. It was awful.

As I drove on further to say my goodbyes to my older son, who was living with his mum and no longer attending church, and to my second-oldest son, who had remained part of our church, a radio announcement came on from the Prime Minister.

Travel was no longer allowed; only special permission would be granted in some instances. It was just like being in a dystopian movie.

To say goodbye to family and friends, knowing this could and almost certainly would be permanent, was extremely traumatic and heartbreaking.

Prophets have to learn to leave things in God's hands. The alternative is to manipulate, like Jezebel, to get our own way, but the Lord wants us to trust him to such an extent that we will even leave our families if the call on our lives requires it.

Jesus, as an adult, went into ministry, and his own family thought he had lost it: "When his family heard about this, they went to take charge of him, for they said, 'He is out of his mind.'" (Mark 3:21 NIV)

When Jesus shockingly demanded: "If anyone comes to Me and does not hate his father and mother, wife and children, brothers and sisters, yes, and his own life also, he cannot be My disciple." (Luke

14:26), He was calling us to live lives that are devoted and subject to Him instead of others, even our family.

We cannot be moved by the opinions of even our nearest and dearest if what they say isn't from the Lord or supported by Scripture. Almost everyone you meet will have an opinion on nearly everything.

In most cases, these opinions concern situations and scenarios they have never even experienced.

Even Christians give this kind of advice and, worse, will often provide advice that is not even biblical.

Many Prophets will never venture to walk out or share the prophecies the Lord desires to speak through their lives because they have become trapped in the desire to please people.

People-pleasing is something the Lord really hates. Jesus Himself said: "...And do not fear those who kill the body but cannot kill the soul. But rather fear Him who is able to destroy both soul and body in hell." (Matthew 10:28)

Paul was clear on how the Lord wanted him to conduct himself and wrote: "Am I now seeking the approval of man, or of God? Or am I trying to please man? If I were still trying to please man, I would not be a servant of Christ" (Galatians 1:10 ESV)

Prophets need to learn to submit to the voice of their Father in heaven, to live to please Him and not be swayed by the nay-sayers in their own families or friendship circles.

Often, we have heard something from the Lord long before others will see it, and we need to bear that in mind when we share the prophetic Word God has spoken to us.

Initially, people may baulk at what we share. Their ego is reacting to being corrected or to not knowing what we seem to know. Their pride is telling them they have it more together than we do, so why should they listen to us? But God has chosen to do things this way.

As we saw right near the beginning of the book, Peter needed to be convinced that Gentiles could be saved and filled with the Spirit, just like the Jews. His frame of reference had to be shifted entirely. He had to be open to a whole new people group. So it is with us.

Despite his triple revelation, Peter later struggled to stick with what he had heard from the Lord and tried to placate the Jews again, but Paul rebuked him openly. (Galatians 2)

If we have heard God, we need to stick with His plan until He says something else.

So many Christians have to 'pay the price' in different ways. We give up our rights and our dreams to follow the call of God on our lives, and oftentimes, we look back and think: *'Was it all worth it?'*

But, as we all believe and hold onto, the truth is that the rewards in heaven for our suffering and sacrifices during this fleeting existence on earth will be far greater: "For our light affliction, which is but for a moment, is working for us a far more exceeding and eternal weight of glory..." (2 Corinthians 4:17) Jesus will reward us for everything we do for Him on this earth.

"For we must all appear before the judgment seat of Christ, so that each one may receive what is due for what he has done in the body, whether good or evil." (2 Corinthians 5:10 ESV)

As we arrived at a darkened, eerily empty Heathrow Airport, it's hard to describe the mix of emotions I felt as I said 'goodbye' to my beloved England and prepared to say 'hello' to my new home on the other side of the planet. It felt like we were on some sort of secret assignment, and in fact, we were. God was not only changing my perspective on life and what 'home' would look like, but He was also shaking up the whole earth as man, in his evil desire to control, spread one of those Revelation plagues across the planet.

Soon, as we kept walking out the 'Noah' Word, we would realise God was making a historic announcement to the world...

As we boarded our Qatar Airlines flight, I thanked the Lord for speaking to me back in January when I booked our tickets. Australian Aviation actually published a piece titled "Last airline standing — Qatar flies 36,000 to and from Australia in April" (Apr 22, 2020), noting that Qatar capitalised on being "one of the last airlines flying regular international routes." This included Australia.

At one point, Qatar's strapline was 'We will get you home', and I felt comforted knowing the Lord truly wanted to create a new home for my family and me in this great country.

After 24 hours of flights and sweaty trudging through airports, we finally arrived in Melbourne, and, as the news channels reported to the rest of the world, we were taken straight into *'quarantine'.*

Even this term held major prophetic significance. 'Quarantine' derives from the Italian *quarantina* or *quaranta giorni,* meaning "forty days."

As I became aware of this, it increasingly seemed that God was indeed speaking about Noah and the 40 days of rain in Noah's time.

I actually stumbled on an article that said that 'Noah' had become the most popular name in that country in 2020, and it turns out that in several other countries in 2020 or 2021, the name 'Noah' had become most popular.

As unlikely as it might seem to most, God was using my family and me to enact a prophetic Word, so He could make the following historic declaration: **"These are the Days of Noah."**

So, I posted this Word on my Facebook page and have declared it ever since, knowing that God had called and confirmed his designation of me as His 'Noah'. Also, I knew that my wife and I had married under the banner of the Rainbow, my family being from just by Noah's Ark and some of hers from a small town called 'Rainbow'. I also knew that we, as a church 'family', had gone into 'the Ark' and then in Melbourne had endured our own version of '40 days' which came in the form of a 14-day 'quarantine', locked inside two adjoining rooms. Not only that, but very soon we would be arriving, or 'landing' if you like, in the Australian version of *Ararat*.

As we had nowhere to live just yet, we initially travelled to Merbein, passing through Ararat, where we stayed for just one night to check it out and look into renting a place there.

We also wanted to briefly consider accepting the job offer as lead pastor of Ararat Community Church before committing to applying for a permanent visa. We were thrilled to find that we both liked the look of the town and that it felt right to all of us.

While in Merbein, I took the chance to prepare my spouse visa application and a bridging visa was granted. We were free to stay, take up the role, and live here permanently. It was amazing how things were falling into place even amid worldwide turmoil.

This prophecy I had walked out and then shared, about us entering into 'The days of Noah', was originally prophesied by Jesus Himself in Luke 17:26, "...as it was in the days of Noah, so it will be also in the days of the Son of Man"

But shortly after I shared it, all of a sudden, many Prophets around the world began to prophesy the exact same Word.

In the UK, just before we left, a nationwide vote of support for our National Health Service (NHS) had begun, with families everywhere putting up stickers in their windows and on their doors that were the actual rainbow symbol with 'NHS' at the bottom. People everywhere were unwittingly participating in God's prophetic Word to the world, that we are officially entering the Last Days.

The rainbow symbol was being reclaimed, even as the world was brought to its knees by humanity's capacity for evil.

The Lord actually gave me a dream regarding COVID, which was centred around a 'World' championship snooker match at the Crucible. We (the world) were 'snookered', but the opponent was doing something 'underhand'. I awoke, realising that, pretty soon, we would discover the virus was the result of underhanded, devious actions rather than anything accidental or natural.

Sure enough, that proved to be the case quite a while later, but God sees the intents and thoughts of man, and He even prophecies what they will do, as we see in the book of Revelation.

The final sign that confirmed we were walking out a modern-day version of Noah going into the ark and landing on Ararat, was the time period between when we entered 'the Ark' and when we officially arrived in Ararat.

Some believers calculate that Noah was in the Ark for 370 days, while others believe there were an additional 7 days after Noah entered the Ark, before the rain started, bringing the total to 377.

As God had timed things, the house we could move into in Ararat was only available from the weekend of May 1st 2020.

There were only two houses available at the time we looked, due to COVID, but this one was better (not right next to the train line) and available when we needed it.

As we had loads of furniture from Dee's parents, stored up for us in Mildura, we needed the trailer and assistance of Dee's sister and brother-in-law. They were working that Friday, so they were only able to come down to Ararat with us on Saturday, 2nd May.

So, we found ourselves officially 'landing' on, or in Ararat, precisely 377 days after our first official entry into 'the Ark', back in the UK, on April 21st 2019. It also turned out that Ararat's postcode was 3 - 377…!

A prophecy that began in 2002, with my parents moving out to the edge of that little hamlet called Noah's Ark in the UK, had finally come to completion eighteen years later on the other side of the planet, as we began a brand-new life in Ararat, Australia.

Chapter 10 - Reflections:

Point 1: God's prophetic Words are spoken by an eternal being who said this through the Apostle Peter: "But, beloved, do not forget this one thing, that with the Lord one day is as a thousand years, and a thousand years as one day." Just because our culture has become a microwave, 'give me a thrill every second' society, does not mean God has changed how He works. He still speaks over decades, centuries even. We are not to demand instant gratification from our eternal, patient and long-suffering God. We need to become like Him.

Point 2: Very often, the Lord will require that we 'lean not on our own understanding' and that we take steps that might not seem logical. Remember, the *Logos* of God includes many stories of faith in which Prophets obey the apparently illogical Word of God. As long as it is His Rhema Word, it will prove to be logical in the end.

Point 3: We can only please God. Let go of trying to please people. They are fickle and flawed just like us, and sooner or later, we will 'fail them'. Focus on pleasing the Lord above everything and everyone else.

Chapter 11: The Challenges

So, we spent a couple of months just being part of the church we were joining before I could officially sign the contract for my new job as Lead Pastor.

During that time, the Lord began to speak to me a prophetic Word for the whole of our church movement. As I have explained already, I often walk out many of the Words God gives me, and as I read the prophecies shared by other Prophets around the world, I always feel sorry for them, knowing they have just been through the very Word they are now sharing.

My first Word to our church movement was both a warning and a Word of wisdom from the Lord. Over and over again, the word 'Spotlight' kept coming up.

As I wrestled with our own church's policy on welcoming 'Persons of Concern' (known, and registered sex offenders) - I realised that 'Spotlight' was a well-known film about the Catholic church and the way they ended up 'in the spotlight', due to some awful offences against children.

As a family, we had moved into a house with no fences, so although it was a nice house with a huge, lovely backyard, we were constantly worried about our children's safety.

As we came from a pretty rough part of London, where stabbings were happening most nights - just down the road - and sexual assaults on adults and children were becoming commonplace, we could not relax knowing that anyone bold enough could simply walk around the side of our house and begin interacting with our children.

The Lord was allowing us to experience a fear that would prompt us to really listen to His voice, and in the process, was giving me a prophetic Word to share with our church movement.

I was aware of several Persons of Concern (POCs) who were already connected to our church, and, after some investigation, realised that a very worrying situation needed to be addressed.

On the day I went to sign my contract, however, I was still struggling with the idea of not allowing any particular group of people to attend our church and felt tempted to 'show mercy' and to continue taking the risk of enabling POCs to come.

I was wrestling with whether I was being too harsh or perhaps fearful. But another shocking situation happened – which I won't share - that shook us to the core, and so that night we accepted that the Lord was saying a very clear: 'No, don't do it'.

I consequently shared this conclusion with our church, and from then on, we no longer allowed POCs to attend. We also addressed the very unsafe situation we had inherited.

Although this upset several people, causing some to leave and a few to no longer be allowed to attend, I knew I had honoured the Lord and obeyed His Voice.

In fact, as is often the case, I realised that the Spotlight reference meant this was not just a Word for me and our local church, but something for our wider movement, so I contacted our own senior leader, who was second in charge of the movement at the time and asked if I could share a prophetic Word. He agreed.

I shared the Word, concluding: "The Lord does not want our movement to end up in the *spotlight* regarding this issue. We need to close the doors to POCs. Does that make any sense to you?"

His response was: "Yes, it does, Jay. We've been discussing this very issue over the last few months and want to reach a decision in time for our National Conference in October. I'll share what you have said with the Board."

Guidance came out shortly after, stating that all of our churches were to desist from allowing POCs to attend. This was to protect the interests of children and vulnerable adults, and, in fact, the Pastors themselves, because recent changes meant our insurance would no longer cover us.

Again, although it was highly uncomfortable and awkward, and meant I had to endure hostility and rejection from a few people, I was privileged to deliver the Word of God Himself on the matter.

We began that first year with extensive outreach, and it certainly seemed we had the finances and the people to 'build' the church. The church grew, and within a year, I had moved up to 4 days of paid employment with the church and had become Senior Pastor with a state credential by July 2021.

Our church also became autonomous, having previously been under the covering of our sister church in Ballarat, and we got on with *doing church* and building relationships in our local town.

On the 12th September 2021, I shared a prophetic Word with our church, which I also shared with our state leadership, that we as the Church should *NOT* fight the particular battle we were facing at the time over vaccinations. At the time, we had a Premier who was enjoying his moment, and the Church felt frustrated and fearful of the pressure it was under. But our God was saying, 'Do not give up your life for the wrong cause.'

The church has often come under great persecution, and in every situation, we, as the Church, need to be discerning and wise in how we respond. Vaccine mandates were implemented in September 2021 and required by October 15th 2021.

I resented being forced into anything, but like Paul—who shook off the snake and was unharmed—I trusted the promise of Scripture that "deadly poison will not hurt them at all," believing God would protect us supernaturally.

In late October 2021, I prophesied to one of our senior leaders: "Although it will look like we are losing power in Victoria, we will actually increase in the power of God." I was referring to the Church.

The next day, the storms hit our state, and the state's biggest-ever power cut occurred.

Australian Disaster Resilience Knowledge Hub wrote: 'On 29 October, over 526,000 households (almost a quarter of all homes in Victoria) suffered power outages; the state's single biggest electricity outage.'

I believed this was a sign from the Lord, given in relation to the increasing attempts by our then State Premier to use emergency 'powers' to maintain a high level of control over us all, particularly the churches.

I consequently shared a prophecy with my peers and, later, with our senior leadership, regarding God's plan that 'Haman' would be 'hung on his own gallows'. (Referring to our esteemed leader, who was known for being immovable from office)

A couple of weeks after I first shared this prophecy, in mid-November 2021, someone protesting against our Premier and his use of emergency powers was seen on the news in Melbourne with his own home-made gallows. I felt this was confirmation.

Sadly, it wouldn't be until September 2023 that our State Premier finally resigned, after a string of personal and political catastrophes led to his downfall. Still, I am confident our prayers helped bring this about, even though for a very long time it seemed he would never be removed from power.

Also, in November 2021, I prophesied again that we, the Church, were in our Nehemiah season – the season after COVID - and that it was 'time to build' or 're-build' as it were.

This Word correlated with many other prophetic words being released from other Prophets around the world, and increasingly, I was finding myself prophesying in my local church, only to find that the exact Word I had shared during the sermon would be prophesied by someone on the other side of the world, the very next day.

In the early months of 2022, I had a dream regarding Russia's invasion of Ukraine.

'Neighbours' (neighbouring countries) of the Bear (Russia) were considering forming alliances with Putin. The dream's message was that they MUST NOT enter into negotiations with him, as he would consume them.

Many Words from the Lord are actually clarion calls for united prayer on a specific issue, and this was one of them.

Around this time, I had a frightening dream from the Lord depicting one of the 'seals' of Revelation coming into effect very 'soon'. (It was rapidly approaching) and it was the 'Seal of War' as seen in the second (red) horse in Revelation 6.

In the dream, I was on board an Australian nuclear submarine, which suddenly dived deep to avoid the impact of the seal.

I know that these submarines are not due to be acquired by us until the early 2030s.

'Soon,' according to God's frame of reference, could be 10 years, rather than 10 weeks. I have long felt that 2030 will be very, very difficult for several reasons, and if that is correct, it would follow that God would prepare us well in advance for what we will be facing.

It is also important to remember that God speaks in His own way and according to His own timetable. We cannot just put our own lens on things and decide what He means, or when He means, on His behalf.

On May 24th 2022, I prophesied again that *"The rain is coming"*. Early in the previous week, Dee had had a dream about storm clouds and then torrential rain, and I felt God wanted me to prophesy this message again.

That Tuesday night, while we were waiting for folks to arrive for Connect group, I suddenly heard a downpour of rain, and thought, *Oh dear, the two ladies who are about to arrive are going to get drenched walking down our driveway.*

A few minutes later, they arrived, bone dry. I looked outside, and there was no rain at all. I sat down to lead the Bible study, thinking, "Wow, that was weird!" *I could hear the rain pouring down, and yet there wasn't any.*

I then had to put that thought on hold and focus on leading our study. Three hours later, the Pastor and Prophet of the church we had finished up at in the UK sent me a video of a well-known Prophet talking about 'the Days of Noah'.

She said in her text message that it reminded her of Dee and me prophetically walking out, Noah landing on Ararat.

In the video she sent me, recorded 11 months earlier, the Prophet explained that on numerous occasions he had supernaturally heard rain pouring down, just like I had. He talked all about this season being the outpouring of the Spirit that is coming.

The following day, two things happened. I visited a member of our church who told me that, not knowing anything about my experience, he had heard rain that morning, thinking it was pouring down, he then checked and discovered he was 'hearing things'...

He, too, had supernaturally heard rain.

And later that day, on May 25th 2022, I opened an emailed prophecy from another US Prophet, entitled "The Rain is Coming."

We have been praying ever since that 'The Rain of the Holy Spirit Would Come'.

In June 2022, at our Pastor's retreat in Horsham, the Lord gave me a dream about one of our up-and-coming leaders who has since become State Chairman. He confirmed its accuracy, and I was blessed to prophesy over and pray for him. This was important because the experience prompted him to invite me to speak at their men's breakfast and to preach at their large church on Sunday morning, 21st August 2022.

In between, in July 2022, the Lord drew my attention to the story of Joseph and as I was also pondering the issue of water supplies in our local area and our propensity to struggle through droughts, I felt the Lord was speaking to me about the possibility of a worldwide drought in the year 2030.

So, on July 17th 2022, I shared this prophetic Word with my local church, suggesting that, just as with Joseph and Egypt's experience, we might have 7 years of plenty, but then 7 years of severe lack, starting in 2030.

At the time, I even mentioned to my congregation that 'I'm just saying, you might want to start storing up resources'. I had begun thinking about how my own family might want to have a borehole dug on our own land to find the water table, believing we may very well face actual drought in 2030.

A week later, the up-and-coming Prophet I mentioned earlier, who now has a considerable following, prophesied the same message, agreeing we will have drought and famine, and as a sign of confirmation, claimed: 'They will say that their rivers have dried up'.

On August 13th 2022, he prophesied again, saying: 'Those who boast in their great rivers, watch how I dry up their watery places'.

In Europe, just after this prophecy, the Danube, Rhine, and Po Rivers reached historic lows in 2022, revealing dry riverbeds.

On 26th September 2022, NBC News aired an article titled "The Rivers Across the Globe Are Under Threat." Detailing how so many rivers across the globe have dried up. They included the Colorado River, the Mississippi River, and the Euphrates, all of which have dried up drastically.

In almost absolute contrast, on August 21st 2022, as I spoke at one of our larger churches, I officially delivered the Word of the Lord that 'the Rain is Coming', meaning the Spiritual rain of the Holy Spirit.

As confirmation, in the natural, the physical rain fell heavily in that next season (Spring 2022 - Victoria-wide).

According to the Bureau of Meteorology (BOM), we had "…the wettest Spring on record", and they went on to say, "Some sites in western Victoria had record-high spring rainfall totals. Specifically, Ararat Prison station (BOM site) recorded a "record highest daily rainfall" for spring (63.0 mm on 28 October) per BOM data."

Ararat is where we live.

Seeing a real-world natural confirmation of the prophetic Word I had delivered again was awesome. To realise that our God is orchestrating events and speaking through natural and supernatural means is really exciting. Although it felt strange to anticipate drought while observing unprecedented downpours, I felt that 7 years would pass quickly and that we should do what we could to prepare.

It was around this time that the Lord gave me a dream regarding someone 'upstairs' at one of our movement's Christian Schools.

'Upstairs' in a dream can represent the mind, or in this context, the 'management' of the organisation.

In the case of a school, the management would be the leadership team or the school board.

In the dream, I had arrived at the school site and, on my way to find the senior leader whom I knew worked there, I overheard a corrupt conversation taking place 'upstairs'.

I knew I needed to share the content of this conversation with the Senior Leader from our church movement as soon as possible. As I was due to go on holiday, I waited a while before contacting him. I was also concerned about being inaccurate, but when I called him, I realised I should have just called him immediately.

The dream was exactly accurate, and it was sent to reassure this leader that his actions in addressing the situation were both correct and necessary.

Having had so many accurate dreams and seen how the Lord reveals secrets to those He trusts, I am always saddened when Christians try to diminish the promise of our Lord, in Acts 2, that states He will indeed speak to us *all* through dreams and visions. In our experience, God is speaking this way all the time. However, He also 'speaks' through natural phenomena...

In 2022, when I first prophesied about the 'rain' coming, a mother and her son, *Noah,* joined our Toddler Church. Then, as I continued to prophesy that 'the rain is coming', a girl named *'Rain'*, with a different spelling, joined us.

Soon after, I realised God wanted us to 'pray like Elijah', as mentioned in James 5, and as confirmation, we had another 'Elijah' join our church. Our little church now had two *Elijahs!*

On one occasion, when I shared a challenging 'Moses Word' — which I had already explained I was bringing — two men named 'Moses' turned up at our church, just for that Sunday!

This Word was a warning from the Lord to keep our hearts right towards leadership, or else He would discipline those in error. I won't share what happened next, but I want to reaffirm that Prophets are often called to correct and challenge believers, and to urge the Church to change course and keep a clean heart, because our Father will discipline those He loves.

Martin Luther was most likely a Prophet. He understood that someone had to stand up and say: 'Enough is Enough. We have drifted from the original faith preached in the New Testament. We need to return to preaching salvation by Grace alone.' Prophets like Luther need to bring correction as the Lord directs.

In 2023, as I began building our house and fighting spiritual battles with one hand, as it were, I again shared that the Church had entered its Nehemiah season. Soon after, a family with a son called 'Nehemiah' joined our church. I had never met a Nehemiah until that point.

The Lord continued to orchestrate things and send people with the relevant name to us, over and over.

While this new season was filled with many positives, privately, I was enduring test after test after test, regarding 'integrity'.

Once, when Dee and I holidayed in the Lake District, years before, I felt the Lord confirming to me that my core value was 'Integrity'.

As we attended a local church that was beginning to move in the Spiritual Gifts, I asked the Lord to confirm that this was His Word for me in that season.

The leader came over to prophesy over me, and after a brief pause, she prophesied: "The Lord says, you are a man of integrity. I feel that so strongly. You are *full* of integrity."

That was beautiful and reassuring to hear the Lord speak to me about myself and my own situation.

Prophets often struggle to hear the Lord for themselves, which is something of an irony. It seems easy to love on others and speak life over them, but, as with other Prophets, we need to rely on input from others, just as people might seek us out for God's Word or confirmation.

I love the idea of *integrity*. Remaining constant, no matter what the temptations are. Staying faithful to the Scriptures, no matter what the pressure is to forsake the Words of our Lord. Being the same authentic self with whoever we are interacting with. I believe all Prophets will face the *integrity test*.

Will they pass it with flying colours, or will they fail and seek compromise, popularity and comfort over authenticity and Truth?

Joseph's integrity was tested. Jeremiah's was too. I could go on and on. They all had to do and say what the Lord was asking, regardless of the way in which they would be received, judged and very often rejected or even tortured and killed.

This has been my own challenge for many years now, especially since 2017. It was at this point that the Lord very clearly spoke to me, saying, 'Satan has asked for you, that he may sift you as wheat.' (Luke 22:31)

Over and over again, the enemy would use people or circumstances to come against my family and me.

Despite all the excitement of God's call on my life to start a church, move to Australia and walk out numerous prophetic Words, I repeatedly found myself in situations where I could not defend myself, and others misrepresented me entirely.

Over and over again, people questioned my motives or projected their own behaviours onto me, expecting I would think in the same way as they did or manipulate as they would. When your core value is integrity, this is particularly grievous.

As we committed to pray for Revival, we came under increasing pressure. I have been physically assaulted on five separate occasions in only a few short years. I have been slandered, mocked, and rejected by groups of people who used to appreciate and respect me.

Then the Lord gave me a dream at the beginning of 2024, which depicted 'Old' mouldy bread being replaced with 'New' fresh bread, and shortly afterwards, a young man with the surname 'New' joined our church.

I understood that the Lord was going to replace those things and people who were 'out of date', meaning that they were not on board with us.

Throughout 2023 and by January 2024, I realised that the Lord was likening my own experience to that of Job in the Bible. Every time I prayed about it, the story came up.

At the beginning of the school year, 2024, as Dee and I officially entered our 'Job season', our son moved schools and became best friends with a 'Job' in his new class. We prepared ourselves for losses.

On May 30th 2024, I prophesied that we as the Church must not tolerate 'Jezebel' and that those who have loved or put up with manipulative people must repent.

God was intending to remove such people from our churches. The following day, a well-known Australian Prophetess shared the very same Word.

Tragically, as Satan took his opportunity to attack us, as he did with Job, and with my older son already estranged, and refusing to contact us or their siblings, Dee and I watched on helplessly as my other son moved away, cut ties and stopped communicating, so that in effect both my sons had 'died to me'.

We grieved as this took place and as our 'cattle and flocks' of church regulars disappeared, due to secret, divisive conversations behind closed doors and what we see as rebellion and dishonour.

At one point, a church regular acted out, pulling a knife out of my back, as she could see what was going on in the spiritual realm.

Before this and still somewhat in 2024, I endured a long season of terrible, sore, red welts and swellings on my skin that hardly anyone knew about. I've been in pain every day for several years now, experiencing strange pains in my side, a numb upper leg, lower back pain, shoulder pain, spasms, and more.

I realise I am getting on in years, but the constant pain and discomfort have added to everything else, just like Job experienced.

Despite numerous prayers from people I know who have great faith, I was not healed and had to endure this season and try to maintain a loving, forgiving attitude, even when I wanted to respond in the flesh. The best lessons we will ever experience are in those seasons of suffering.

How can you learn to love and forgive your enemies if you don't have any? How can you learn to forgive and honour those who might not deserve it, unless you are dishonoured and mistreated along the way and have to choose not to respond in like manner? How can you learn to have integrity unless you are tempted to give up, give in and give over all that you have to the enemy?

On the 3rd and 5th December 2024, I had two dreams from the Lord indicating that our 'enemy' might cut our national power, communication and data lines as an act of war.

Three months later, on 20th February 2025, the BBC ran an article that led with: *'Shortly after midday local time on Christmas Day 2024, workers at the Finnish electricity company Fingrid noticed the main* undersea electricity cable linking Finland with Estonia was damaged, significantly reducing Estonia's power supply.'

The article went on to say: "Certainly the authorities in Finland are not alone in their suspicions regarding Russia and subsea cable infrastructure. In November 2024, Russian surveillance ship, the Yantar, was spotted "loitering over UK critical undersea infrastructure", according to the Defence Secretary, John Healey. In January 2025 it apparently happened again, with the Royal Navy monitoring the Yantar, which the Ministry of Defence said was being used "for gathering intelligence and mapping the UK's underwater infrastructure"."

Then, in July 2025, 7 News ran an article about how our nation, Australia, is vulnerable to cyberattack. They explained that before a land war, our enemy could cut our data cables.

One quote said: "It would be in cyber. You'd start to see a degradation of the internet." Australia's vulnerability is stark: 99 per cent of our internet traffic travels through just 15 undersea cables."

Prior to the two dreams and these news articles, I had no understanding of cables on the seafloor, what they were there for, or how another country might sabotage them as an act of war, but God did, and again He chose to share that warning with me.

Despite the awful struggle we were having dealing with several Jezebel spirits and the full onslaught of the enemy against our church and my beautiful family, the Lord continued to speak to me about international events.

I would have preferred not to have gone through the horrendous pain of betrayal and backstabbing that took place over that year and partly into 2025, but that is the test the Lord had set, and that is the way He planned to speak His message to the church as we head into 2026.

Like Job, we had to lose everything and hang onto Jesus. We had to endure the advice of Job's *friends*, too.

I'll unpack this prophetic Word in our final chapter, but here is the Rhema Word of God for this season of the Church in 2026:

The Lord wants to give us double, just like He did with Job. He wants to pour out His Spirit on us and bless us, but He will not contend with man.

Chapter 11 - Reflections:

Point 1: As Prophets develop their gifting and become more accurate and discerning regarding what God is saying, who He is saying it to, and when He wants it to be said, God will begin to confirm His calling on our lives, even to the most cynical of believers around us.

Point 2: Our integrity as Prophets will be tested in every way, so hold fast to what the Lord says about you in Scripture. Refuse to behave in such a way that is two-faced or carnal. Remain authentic and consistent. We are to be *in* the world, but not *of* the world, so refuse to capitulate to the ways of the world.

Point 3: Allow the Lord to trim off unfruitful branches from our own lives and our ministries. Don't just do what everyone else is doing; see what the Father is doing and do that.

Chapter 12: The Consultation

Like Job, we can be tempted to look around us and believe that the good health of our churches or the attendance figures we get excited about are largely down to our own efforts, and, as Dee and I had to learn, to some extent, that is true. People can come to church because we put a lot of effort into relationships, presentation, or both. Pursuing 'excellence'. They come to church because they are impressed by the service, the warm welcome, or the music. They play along, doing *the Christian thing* in the Christian bubble, but never actually become *disciples*.

As long as we don't offend them, they'll keep coming. As long as we never challenge their behaviour or character flaws, they will joyfully sing our praises.

However, when the Devil comes calling, with something 'better', off they go, because they are *consumer Christians*. They come to receive rather than to give, and they have never learned to 'die to self' and commit themselves to the Kingdom effort.

Tragically, very often, Pastors are hopelessly playing a delicate game of 'don't rock the boat'. Trying to keep people on side, hoping not to offend them in any way, knowing that this narcissistic tendency of our prevailing culture will mean anyone at any point could drop us and go to another, less challenging and more liberal church, just down the road.

This culture is not what we find in the New Testament. This culture is what *we* have created, or at least *tolerated*. It produces converts who have no integrity whatsoever.

As they return to the workspace on a Monday morning, they immediately revert back to their other persona and forget all about Jesus until the following Sunday morning. They behave just like their peers, never mentioning church, the Bible, or, God forbid, *Jesus!*

They have not *crucified the flesh*, and we have enabled them to stay that way.

We might have a church of 50+, which we've grown from just 15 and think, *'Well, we're doing pretty well, considering the circumstances and the town we live in.'*

We might have a much bigger church and have planted several campuses, and we could find ourselves thinking, *'We have become really efficient and organised, we're doing a great job."*

The Truth is, however, that Church attendance in the Western world has been on the decline for decades. Although the Pentecostal Church might be growing a bit, it is not growing anywhere near fast enough to change our country or save over half of the population, who are currently on *the wide road that leads to destruction*.

We, the Apostles, Prophets, Evangelists, and Teachers, are all responsible for this current state of affairs. And as Job experienced, these flocks may well be wiped out initially, until we accept, as he did: "The LORD gave, and the LORD has taken away; Blessed be the name of the LORD." (Job 1:21)

Job realised, as we need to, that *EVERYTHING* good we have is from the Lord. We cannot take the credit for *anything*.

In fact, we must get back to *doing church* the way God modelled for us in the book of Acts, in the Fear of the Lord and with humility.

We need to repent of trying to 'do church' without the manifest Presence and Power of the Holy Spirit, and return to praying with all our hearts for the lost and for His Presence to fill our churches.

Our preaching needs to revert to that timeless message of repentance, saturated in Truth and Grace, just as Jesus, Peter, James, John, and Paul all taught. Then, as the Lord promises, as we humble ourselves and pray, He "will hear from heaven, and will forgive their sin and heal their land." (2 Chronicles 7:14)

We need to wake up out of our spiritual slumber and allow the Lord to break our hearts again for the lost who, at this very minute, are piling into hell in their droves.

If we can ask the hard questions and allow the Lord to kill off all our selfish ambition and pride, there is still a chance that we might corporately begin to cry out to the Lord in prayer and eventually experience a national and international Revival.

But we have to reach the point where we are willing to petition Him continually, without giving up, until we get the breakthrough and until we have His Presence. (Luke 18:1-8) We need to be willing to spend hours in prayer, interceding for our towns, regions, states, and nations.

We need to approach this upcoming season of Church History with the same urgency Elijah demonstrated during the famine in his land, and pray as he did for the rain. The 'rain' for us signifies an unprecedented outpouring of the Holy Spirit, and boy, do we need it.

More often than not, prayer has become a side note we squeeze in for five minutes because we don't want to bore our faithful attendees, and because prayer is costly, most of us avoid it.

Yet if we pause and truly consider it, prayer should be the number one activity in every church. *Pentecost* came after concerted prayer.

Without Prophets, we can completely overlook a vital call like this to return to prayer. Prophets are needed because they bring us back to the fundamentals.

Without Prophets, we can be clueless as to what the Lord wants to do in response to the rise of unbiblical ideologies, secularism, satanism and false religions. Prophets bring the strategies we need, straight from Heaven.

As I mentioned earlier, I have only recently prophesied that God wants to raise up Godly leaders to take on influential roles in Government and every committee across the land. If this is true, who will step forward? Who will dedicate themselves to sharpening their skills, seek God's favour, and play the long game to attain positions of influence like Joseph, Esther, or Daniel and his friends?

Without the input of Prophets, we may continue operating like worldly organisations rather than functioning as the model churches of Jerusalem and Antioch, which *sent out* much-needed resources and people to build up the smaller churches.

We might dismiss the fact that smaller churches are 'failing' and blame the disheartened pastor or leaders, reasoning that God has clearly changed His mind about the church He once inspired an Apostle to plant and let it close. We do this even though the early church 'shared all their resources' (I paraphrase), so that 'There were no needy persons among them'. *We,* on the other hand, will even invite gifted young folks from smaller churches to join our already thriving church, knowing that the smaller churches have no one else.

We fill our rosters with all the people and resources another church needs because we want to strengthen our own church and let the 'poor' church handle its own issues. (Luke 3:11 / 1 John 3:17). But Paul wrote this to the churches: "For I do not mean that others should be eased and you burdened; but by an equality, that now at this time your abundance may supply their lack, that their abundance also may supply your lack—that there may be equality." (1 Corinthians 8:13-14)

The early church was focused on strengthening *every* church, with multiple leaders moving around and staying for periods of time, to build them up: Paul, Silas, Timothy, Apollos, Barnabus, John Mark, Titus, Epaphroditus, Priscilla and Aquila, Agabus, Judas, and John.

We need to completely reshape the idea of ministry, so that the next generation is willing to be 'sent' by the Holy Spirit. (Acts 13:2–4) And willing to 'train' by serving where they are needed!

Without Prophets, we might be unaware of how to navigate AI taking over large portions of jobs, which could lead to a significant drop in giving. We may keep our heads in the sand and never even stop to consider: *What is God's plan for funding our buildings or the wages of the pastors and leaders, as this crisis unfolds?*

We may ignore the impending control of digital IDs, national digital currencies, and the very real possibility that Christians with perspectives that are not 'tolerated' will 'not be able to buy or sell'.

Instead of seeking God's wisdom and collaborating with other Christians and churches on how we will respond, we claim, 'God will take care of us, no need to worry!' But 'not worrying' and planning ahead are not the same. God expects us to plan.

God sends 'Josephs', even to foreign nations like Egypt, because whoever will receive a Prophet will receive a Prophet's reward.

Without Prophets, we might never have thought about how to feed orphans and widows during times of famine, drought, and war—all while we focus on preaching the Bible, leaving our congregants to work it all out for themselves. But God knows what we need to know, and He will speak through His Prophets, if we will listen.

Over the past 2 years, despite the economic challenges and having only one full-time and one part-time income, I have built a paid-off house, meaning we only need to clear the mortgage on the land.

We now own a highly valuable asset that cost us a fraction of the usual price, with much less interest paid to the banks. It is also 12000mm x 12000mm, and has 12 doors - modelled on the New Jerusalem, which I hope we will get to see with our own eyes in this lifetime. The Lord led us through this entire process, providing for us in every way as we followed the prophetic Rhema Word of God we had received and took an unconventional, Spirit-led approach.

Wisdom and revelation are available to all who will listen to the Prophets that Jesus is sending in this hour. We need to believe God wants to *equip us for every good work* and in every situation.

However, we cannot afford to just 'do church' the conventional way anymore. Thousands, millions even, are dying and going to hell, just because they're not willing to attend one of our amazing events.

We need to intercede with groanings, heartbroken at the loss of so many. We need to remove our smug satisfaction at achieving another 'good service' and find the compassion that moved Jesus to reach the lost.

My prayer is that we will return to the biblical model of church and humble ourselves enough to witness a great Revival sweep across Australia and the world. That we will experience an outpouring of our Lord's Power and Presence that will be irresistible to the masses as our fervent prayers bring the rain. I pray that we will return to honouring Prophets and give them a chance to speak, rather than dismiss every concern as conspiracy or fear-mongering.

God wants to give us strategies. Wisdom. Favour and positions of influence. And He will tell us how, through His Prophets.

We should even be developing schools of the Prophets to foster character formation and increased accuracy and wisdom in applying the *Rhema* Word of God to any and every situation the Church and individuals will encounter in these Last Days.

And like Job, we should be wrestling with the Lord as Satan enjoys his moment, knowing that as long as we keep a good heart, as he did, pray without giving up, as Elijah did, then the Holy Spirit will pour Himself out on us and give us back many times what we have lost.

Where are all the Prophets? They are right there in front of us, sitting in every congregation, spread throughout every sphere of life, waiting to speak. We would do well to repent of quenching the Holy Spirit from flowing through His Prophets and seek them out as soon as possible.

May our Lord Jesus be given all the glory as Prophets and Evangelists are released to minister in the Spirit, and we as a mature Church body begin to function as we should: with unity, passion, commitment and integrity.

May we pursue the heart of our Father in Heaven, the Face of our wonderful Lord Jesus and the beautiful Presence and Power of the Holy Spirit with everything we've got, believing with all our hearts that His will is that *'none should perish'*.

May we honour one another, receiving Prophets as we would receive Jesus and gaining the Prophet's reward that comes with the Word of God they are bringing.

May we love our Lord with actions, not merely words, as we seek to go out and make authentic, Christlike disciples. *Amen*

Chapter 12 - Reflections:

Point 1: If God in His infinite wisdom has decided to speak to His church and the nations through Prophets – how can we better facilitate them sharing His Word? How can we ensure our churches better reflect the model churches in the New Testament, with schools for the Prophets and a willingness to 'send out' ministry to strengthen other churches?

Point 2: If Jesus sat down with us today and asked, "How have you been receiving the Prophets that I've been sending your way? How would we respond? Do we even know who the Prophets are in our own congregations and church movements?

Point 3: What are the Prophets saying about the next 10 years? How can we respond so that we can still be here, building the Kingdom as one united Church Body, when Jesus returns?

Acknowledgements:

First and foremost, I want to thank my Lord and Saviour Jesus Christ, who has been faithful to speak, patient to teach, and steadfast in confirming His Word to me over many years. This book exists only because He first spoke and then called me to write.

I am deeply grateful to my family, whose love, patience, and support have sustained me through seasons of uncertainty, delay, and sacrificial obedience. Your willingness to stand with me, even when the path was unclear, has been a constant source of strength.

I also wish to thank the pastors, leaders, and mentors who have empowered me to prophesy and who have modelled what it means to steward responsibility within the Church faithfully. Your guidance has helped shape not only my ministry but also my character.

Finally, I acknowledge the broader Body of Christ. It is my prayer that this book would not divide, but serve—to provoke reflection, encourage listening, and help create space once again for the Holy Spirit to speak freely through His Prophets.

Book Recommendations:

Surprised by the Voice of God — Jack Deere
The God Chasers — Tommy Tenney
Finding God — Dr Larry Crabb
Understanding Dreams and Visions — John Paul Jackson
Unmasking the Jezebel spirit — John Paul Jackson
Needless Casualties of War — John Paul Jackson
The Bait of Satan — John Bevere
Good or God — John Bevere
The Power of a Whisper — Bill Hybels
Just Walk Across the Room — Bill Hybels
The Christian Atheist — Craig Groeschel
Mere Christianity — C.S. Lewis
The Normal Christian Life — Watchman Nee
The Heavenly Man — Brother Yun
Insanity of God — Nik Ripken

www.ingramcontent.com/pod-product-compliance
Lightning Source LLC
Chambersburg PA
CBHW071241070526
44583CB00017B/2275